D0127725

YEAR 'ROUND ACTIVITIES FOR FOUR-YEAR-OLD CHILDREN

Anthony J. Coletta, Ph.D.

Associate Professor of Early Childhood Education
William Paterson College, Wayne, New Jersey

Kathleen Coletta

Illustrated by Margie Tuohy Jordan

THE CENTER FOR APPLIED RESEARCH IN EDUCATION, INC., WEST NYACK, NEW YORK

© 1986 by
THE CENTER FOR APPLIED
RESEARCH IN EDUCATION, INC.

West Nyack, N.Y.

All rights reserved.

Permission is given for individual
preschool teachers and directors to
reproduce the Skills–Concepts Checklist
and activity patterns for classroom use.
Reproduction of these materials for an
entire school system is strictly forbidden.

To our brothers and sisters:
Joe, Rick, Laura, Carolann, and Gregory

Library of Congress Cataloging-in-Publication Data

Coletta, Anthony J.
   Year 'round activities for four-year-old children.

   (Preschool curriculum activities library)
   Includes bibliographical references.
   1. Education, Preschool—Curricula.   2. Creative
activities and seat work.   3. Play.   4. Child
development—Evaluation—Forms.   I. Coletta, Kathleen.
II. Title.   III. Title: Year around activities for
four-year-old children.   IV. Series: Coletta, Anthony J.
Preschool curriculum activities library.
LB1140.4.C644   1986   372.5   85-30934

ISBN 0-87628-983-9

Printed in the United States of America

ABOUT THE AUTHORS

Anthony J. Coletta, Ph.D., is presently associate professor of Early Childhood Education at William Paterson College (Wayne, New Jersey), where he teaches Early Childhood Education courses. The holder of a Montessori teaching certificate, Dr. Coletta has taught at all levels, preschool to junior high, working with both gifted and learning disabled preschool and primary children.

Kathleen Coletta, B.A., Early Childhood Education, is an experienced preschool teacher and currently serves as the Director of the Ponds Valley Preschool in Oakland, New Jersey. She has also served as a consultant to other area preschools developing curriculum manuals, newsletters, and a parent-education program.

ACKNOWLEDGMENTS

We thank . . .

. . . **Margie Tuohy Jordan** for painstakingly reviewing each activity so that our ideas could be accurately depicted in her drawings. We also appreciate her creative suggestions.

. . . **Michelle Lyons** for typing all three manuscripts with accuracy, efficiency, and patience.

. . . **Donna Reid and the staff** of the Donna Reid Child Development Center, Franklin Lakes, New Jersey, for encouraging and implementing our curriculum plan as it was developed and giving us continuous feedback, criticisms, and suggestions. The teachers who cooperated during the field testing were Kathy Tenkate, Linda Fitzsimmons, Lois Wallace, Lori Doda, Rose Silvestri, and Emily Lio.

. . . **Bob Messano** for his original songs.

. . . **John Sheehan and Kevin DeFreest** for their musical arrangements.

. . . **Faith Geruldsen, LeAnn Bucco, and Dawn Ciarleglio,** graduate students at William Paterson College, Wayne, New Jersey, for assisting with the research of books, fingerplays, records, and poetry that enhanced our curriculum and for contributing their own teaching ideas.

. . . **William Strader,** doctoral candidate in early childhood education at the University of Massachusetts, Amherst, Massachusetts, for contributing many suggestions based on his extensive experience as a preschool teacher and director.

. . . **Alpha Caliandro,** associate professor of early childhood education at William Paterson College, for guiding our selections of classical music pieces recommended in the activities.

. . . **Dr. Laura Aitken, Dr. Marge Moreno, and Joan Heins,** faculty of Early Childhood Education at William Paterson College, for their astute observations and recommendations regarding parts of the manuscript.

We further wish to acknowledge those traditional nursery rhymes, action songs, and fingerplays for which no authors have been located and that appear in many other books.

CHARACTERISTICS OF FOUR-YEAR-OLD CHILDREN

Four-year-old children are lively and adventurous, and they burst with motor activity. Like two- and three-year-olds, they are egocentric and are perceptual thinkers, unable to think logically or abstractly. Although 40 percent of their play is sensory-motor* (free movement of large and small muscles), 30 percent is symbolic and is demonstrated largely through socio-dramatic play that involves taking on roles and verbally interacting with other children. Such play is made possible by the expansion of spoken language in the fourth year: 1500 words in early four-year-olds and more than 2000 in five-year-olds.** They can speak readily in sentences of ten or more words.

Four-year-old children exhibit increased cognitive skills by asking more questions and showing greater curiosity about the environment. There is great interest in the printed word, especially their names; and their attention span has increased to enable them to listen to a story of approximately ten minutes in length. In addition, four-year-olds have the ability to predict events and outcomes of stories.

Like three-year-olds, four-year-old children are magical thinkers. Their egocentricity causes them to create events and perceive their abilities as limitless. For example, a typical four-year-old might say, "I have X-ray vision. I can see through anything!" Like three-year-olds, four-year-old children also continue to think animistically—that is, they give human characteristics to inanimate objects.

Physically, four-year-old children can move their bodies more creatively and are in greater control, being able to stop upon a teacher's command or the termination of music. Their fine motor abilities have improved their artistic skills, allowing them to draw a human figure with major body parts and facial features.

These and many other characteristics are classified under the areas of cognitive, language, self, social studies, math, science, and gross and fine motor movements and are listed in the Skills–Concepts Checklist for Four-Year-Olds. These one hundred skills and concepts are sequentially presented and systematically developed in the children through carefully planned activities for September through June.

Using this book will save you a significant amount of time that would normally be allotted to short- and long-term curriculum planning. More important, the time you spend teaching children will be used more effectively. Please refer to the following section for specific suggestions for using this book, the Checklist, and the activities.

* Charles F. Wolfgang, *Growing and Learning Through Play*. (New York: McGraw-Hill, 1981).
** Margaret Lay-Dopyera and John Dopyera, *Becoming a Teacher of Young Children*, 2nd ed. (Lexington, Mass.: D. C. Heath, 1982).

SKILLS–CONCEPTS CHECKLIST*
FOR FOUR-YEAR-OLDS
(Developmental Characteristics)

A child who is 48 to 60 months of age typically demonstrates a large increase in vocabulary and physical abilities. The following abilities will emerge as the child approaches age five. The activities within this book have been designed to develop the skills and concepts listed below in a manner consistent with the child's needs and interests. Monitor the child's progress and evaluate it twice during the school year by placing a check (√) next to the skill or concept once it has been mastered.

Name _____ Birthdate _____

COGNITIVE

Personal Curiosity/Autonomy	JAN.	JUNE
1. Shows an increasing curiosity and sense of adventure		
2. Asks an increasing number of questions		
3. Takes initiative in learning		
4. Shows an interest in the printed word		
5. Pays attention and concentrates on a task		

Senses		
6. Demonstrates accurate sense of touch ("thick" or "thin") and smell		
7. Describes foods by taste (sweet, sour, and salty)		
8. Reproduces a simple pattern of different items from memory		
9. Ranks sounds (loud, louder, loudest; soft, softer, softest)		
10. Observes objects and pictures closely		

Memory		
11. Recalls information previously taught		

Logical Thinking		
12. Interprets the main idea of a story		
13. Orders pictures by time sequence to tell a story		

Relationships		
14. Makes a simple comparison of two objects in terms of difference ("How are a cat and dog different?") and sameness ("How are a cat and dog alike?")		
15. Completes a statement of parallel relationships		

Predicting		
16. Predicts what will happen next in a story or situation		
17. Predicts realistic outcomes of events ("What will happen if we go on a picnic?")		

* This checklist was developed from the *Skill–Concept Development Checklists for Two Through Five Year Olds* (St. Louis County, Missouri: Parent–Child Early Education). Developed by the Ferguson–Florissant School District. Parts reprinted with their permission.

© 1986 by The Center for Applied Research in Education, Inc.

© 1986 by The Center for Applied Research in Education, Inc.

Creativity	JAN.	JUNE
18. Responds well to nondirective questions ("How many ways can you think of to move across the room?")		
19. Proposes alternative ways of doing art experiences, movement activities, and story endings		
20. Represents thoughts in pictures		
21. Draws a human figure with major body parts		
22. Participates verbally or nonverbally in imaginative play or puppetry (socio-dramatic play)		
23. Acts out a familiar story or nursery rhyme as the teacher recites		

Comments:

LANGUAGE

Sentence Structure

	JAN.	JUNE
24. Speaks in six, eight, ten, or more words		
25. Makes relevant verbal contributions in small group discussion		
26. Shows understanding of past, present, and future tenses by using proper verb form		
27. Verbalizes songs and fingerplays		
28. Dictates own experience stories		
29. Describes a simple object using color, size, shape, composition, and use		
30. Describes a picture with three statements		

Listening

31. Listens to directions for games and activities		
32. Listens to stories of at least ten minutes in length		
33. Retells five-sentence short story in sequence using own words		
34. Understands prepositions		

Labeling

35. Labels common everyday items such as clothing, animals, and furniture		
36. Orally labels pictures and drawings ("That's a dog.")		

Letter/Word Recognition

37. Verbally identifies letters in first name (and subsequently in last name)		
38. Identifies many letters of the alphabet		
39. Distinguishes words that begin with the same sound (*book/boy*)		
40. Names two words that rhyme in a group of three (*tie, road, pie*)		
41. Supplies a rhyming word to rhyme with a word given by the teacher		
42. Associates a letter with its sound in spoken words		

Comments:

SELF	**JAN.**	**JUNE**
43. Touches, names, and tells function of parts of the body (head, eyes, hands, arms, feet, legs, nose, mouth, ears, neck, trunk, ankle, knee, shoulder, wrist, elbow, and heel)		
44. Verbalizes full name, address, age, birthday, and telephone number		
45. Identifies expressions of feelings		
46. Feels good about self and abilities		

Comments:

SOCIAL STUDIES

Interpersonal

	JAN.	**JUNE**
47. Shows empathy toward other children		
48. Works cooperatively with adults		
49. Works and plays cooperatively with other children		

Concepts

50. Begins to understand that problems can be solved by talking and not fighting		
51. Understands that we wear appropriate clothing to protect us from extremes of weather		
52. Understands that families share responsibilities of work and recreation		
53. Begins to understand the importance of keeping the school surroundings clean and free from litter		

Comments:

MATH

Counting

	JAN.	**JUNE**
54. Counts from 1 to _____		
55. Understands ordinal positions first through fifth		
56. Recognizes and orders the cardinal numerals in sequence		
57. Solves simple verbal problems using numerals ("If you have two pieces of candy and I give you one more, how many will you have?")		

Classifying

58. Classifies objects by color, size, shape, and texture		

Size Differences

59. Orders and compares size differences (big, bigger, biggest; small, smaller, smallest; short, shorter, shortest; long, longer, longest)		

Shapes

60. Points to and names: triangle, circle, square, rectangle, and diamond		

© 1986 by The Center for Applied Research in Education, Inc.

© 1986 by The Center for Applied Research in Education, Inc.

Quantitative Concepts	**JAN.**	**JUNE**
61. Distinguishes between concepts of "some," "most," and "all"		
62. Compares objects as to weight ("Which is heavier?" "Which is lighter?")		
63. Understands concepts of "full," "half full," and "empty"		
64. Understands fractions (½, ¼, whole)		

Sets

65. Identifies a set as a collection of objects having a common property		
66. Establishes a one-to-one correspondence through matching members of equivalent sets (matching six cowboys to six cowboy hats)		
67. Distinguishes between equivalent and non-equivalent sets through matching		
68. Understands that each number is one more than the preceding number ("What is one more than two?")		
69. Identifies an empty set as one having no members		

Comments:

SCIENCE

Concepts

70. Understands that each animal needs its own kind of food and shelter		
71. Understands that plants need water, light, warmth, and air to live		
72. Understands that many foods we eat come from seeds and plants		
73. Understands that some things float in water and some things sink in water		
74. Understands the balance of nature—that is, animals need to eat plants, vegetables, and insects in order to live		
75. Understands that plant life, animal life, and other aspects of the environment must be respected		

Colors

76. Points to and names colors		

Comments:

GROSS MOTOR

Arm–Eye Coordination

77. Catches a ball away from body with hands only (large ball/small ball)		
78. Throws a ball or beanbag with direction		
79. Throws a ball into the air and catches it by self		
80. Bounces and catches a ball		

Body Coordination	JAN.	JUNE
81. Walks forward and backward on a line ten feet long without stepping off		
82. Walks a line heel-to-toe eight feet long without stepping off		
83. Balances on foot for five seconds		
84. Stops movement activity upon teacher's direction		
85. Moves body creatively upon teacher's direction		
86. Claps with music		

Rhythm

	JAN.	JUNE
87. Claps and marches in time with music		
88. Responds to rhythms with appropriate body movements		

General Movement

	JAN.	JUNE
89. Produces the following motions: walks backwards, runs smoothly, marches, skips, gallops, hops four times on each foot, walks heel-to-toe, and walks and runs on tiptoe		

Comments:

_____		
_____		
_____		

FINE MOTOR

Finger Strength and Dexterity

	JAN.	JUNE
90. Folds and creases paper two times		
91. Folds paper into halves, quarters, and diagonals		

Eye-Hand Coordination

	JAN.	JUNE
92. Strings ten small beads		
93. Follows a sequence of holes when lacing		
94. Works a puzzle of ten or more pieces		
95. Uses crayon or pencil with control within a defined area		
96. Connects a dotted outline to make a shape		
97. Follows a series of dot-to-dot numerals, 1–10, to form an object		
98. Reproduces shapes (circle, square, triangle, and rectangle)		
99. Controls brush and paint		
100. Uses scissors with control to cut along a straight line and a curved line		

Comments:

_____		
_____		
_____		

© 1986 by The Center for Applied Research in Education, Inc.

ABOUT THE
PRESCHOOL CURRICULUM ACTIVITIES LIBRARY

Year 'Round Activities for Four-Year-Old Children is the third volume of three in the *Preschool Curriculum Activities Library.* This *Library* represents a multisensory developmental approach to curriculum development for two-, three-, and four-year-old children. The activities presented stimulate the senses of sight, touch, hearing, smell, and taste, while being appropriate to the children's stages of development. Several important research models provide a foundation for creative lesson plans that help you solve the major organizational problem in early childhood education—matching developmentally appropriate daily activities to traditional preschool topics.

In this *Library,* the major work of building a preschool curriculum has been done for you. Topics, skills, and concepts that have been "matched" to the proper stage of the child's growth are included in all the activities. Topics in the form of themes and sub-themes have been carefully identified and ordered and are based on seasonal interest. A total of 585 activities are described in the three-book *Library,* and each one is based on skills identified in the Checklists for two-, three-, and four-year-old children.

More important, each book of the *Preschool Curriculum Activities Library* has been field tested to provide you with a complete developmental program. In addition, **Developmental Skills-Concepts Checklists*** are included for this age group as well as the other two age groups in the *Library.* (See the Complete Preschool Development Plan at the back of the book.) Each Checklist is an individual skills record that outlines the abilities you can reasonably expect from children at each age.

The following uses are recommended for the preceding Skills-Concepts Checklist for Four-Year-Olds found on pages vi-x:

- Assess a child's skill and concept ability levels. This information of children's strengths and/or deficiencies can help modify curriculum plans by creating or changing activities.

- Monitor a child's progress throughout the year. Duplicate the Checklist for each child and keep it in his or her folder. Supplement the Checklist evaluations with anecdotal statements. It is recommended that the Checklist be completed twice yearly, in January and June.

- Use the Checklist as a progress report to parents and as a reference during parent conferences. Specific statements rather than broad generalizations can be made. Parents who are concerned about skill-concept development will be assured that their children will not miss any major topics, concepts, or skills.

- Use to individualize instruction by grouping children with a common strength or weakness. Teaching one lesson to a small group needing similar skill development saves the teacher's time and energy.

- Give the Checklist to the child's teacher next year. He or she will then know what skills the child has been exposed to and can more easily plan reinforcement and extension.

*The Skills-Concepts Checklist was originally developed by Dr. Walter Hodges of Georgia State University, Atlanta, Georgia, while he was working as a consultant with the Ferguson-Florissant schools in Ferguson, Missouri. The Checklist has been further modified by the authors to include the findings of other early childhood authorities, notably Dr. Carol Seefeldt, *A Curriculum for Preschools,* 2nd ed. (Columbus, O.: Chas. E. Merrill, 1980); Dr. Joseph Sparling, *Learningames for the First Three Years* (New York: Walker and Co., 1979); and Dr. Charles F. Wolfgang, *Growing and Learning Through Play* (New York: McGraw-Hill, 1981).

- Use the Checklist to understand the total development of children as they pass through the preschool years. The Checklist can also be used for inservice training, parent workshops, or orienting new staff members.
- Use a checkmark (√) to keep track of those skills mastered by the children. With this simple checking system, you can quickly scan the Checklist, noting the skills and concepts required. These skills and concepts can be reinforced as part of routine activities as you desire.

Each skill or concept has been carefully integrated into the curriculum. You know that the differences among two-, three-, and four-year-olds are more impressive than among seven-, eight-, and nine-year-olds. The Checklist provides a justification for creating differentiated learning experiences with classes of two-, three-, and four-year-olds. It can easily be reproduced for use in individual record keeping, as a progress report to parents, and as a tool for individualizing instruction.

Monthly themes and weekly subthemes of high interest are included as part of a unit approach to curriculum development. Within the unit framework, an entire preschool can study a broad topic for one month, separated into four related areas or weekly subthemes. The five activities within each subtheme are organized to develop and reinforce the skills and concepts found on the Skills-Concepts Checklist.

The ten themes and thirty-nine subthemes, one for each month and week of the school year, were created with the following concepts in mind:

1. Learning begins with the selection of topics that are most familiar to children and gradually expands into areas that are more challenging.
2. Good teaching involves creative long- and short-range planning. Within a well-organized framework, teachers can follow the child's lead and expand on his or her interests.
3. A thematic approach to curriculum development is most effective when the themes are highly related to the immediate environment surrounding the child.

Every effort has been made to connect topics to the seasonal events children will see and hear about each month. While this is not a holiday curriculum, some holidays are included in the subthemes and activities. For example, the November theme, "Home and Family," is strongly related to the meaning of Thanksgiving. Religious holidays, however, are not included within the themes and subthemes. Such holidays should be observed by each school in a manner appropriate to local cultural traditions.

195 ready-to-use activities are described for an entire school year of thirty-nine weeks (or ten months). Along with a multisensory emphasis, many physical movement suggestions are included to help children explore each topic as an active participant, at his or her own pace.

The activities can be used either with a whole group or in small groups. Whenever possible, you should aim to accomplish the activities in small groups or individually. Each activity, one for each day of the school year, includes the skill or concept to be learned, behavioral objectives, materials needed, a step-by-step procedure, and ways to vary or extend the activity.

Each of the thirty-nine subthemes contains five activities selected from the subject areas described here. Read the activities before trying them, so that materials such as books, records, posters, puzzles, and other recommended resources can be located or ordered, and the activities can be modified to best meet the needs of the children you teach.

By using these activities as a springboard, you can create challenging and involving activities that can be easily integrated into any existing educational framework.

The following subject areas are covered in the *Preschool Curriculum Activities Library:*

Language Arts. The language arts activities in this curriculum follow a language experience approach. The children's receptive and expressive language is enhanced through the use of fingerplays, nursery rhymes, poetry, discussions, and experience charts. Furthermore, many fine books for children are suggested, including Caldecott Medal and Honor books.

There are no formal reading or writing experiences among the 195 activities. Such experiences are appropriate for the concrete stage of development, ages seven to eleven. Stimulating experiences, along with the manipulation of objects, are much more important for preschoolers than ditto sheets and workbook activities.

Science. The science activities are aimed at encouraging observation, comparison, exploration, testing, inquiry, and problem solving. Within many activities, children's senses are stimulated. You can help them notice cause and effect, as well as keep simple records.

Nutrition/Foods Experience. With the nutrition activities, children learn about group cooperation, weights and measures, time, and changes of matter from one form to another. Moreover, they develop an understanding of how to follow directions in sequence, gain pleasure from creating simple foods, and develop good eating habits.

Creative Dramatics/Movement. Creative dramatics aid children in developing language and spontaneous play. Creative dramatics can take many forms, such as creative movement (in which children use sensory-motor abilities and gain skill in body control), rhythm, tempo, timing, following directions, and group cooperation. While involved in creative dramatics, children sometimes use concrete objects as symbols, and you can extend their play to include pantomime, story dramatizations, role playing, and puppetry.

Social Studies. The social studies activities focus on learning about self, home, family, transportation, and the immediate as well as the larger community. Emphasis is on the children's involvement in their own learning. Therefore, field trips to local sites are an important part of the curriculum. The Variations/Ways to Extend sections of several lessons suggest inviting parents and other community people into the classroom to share their special talents and information.

Art. Art for preschoolers is a creative process that allows for choice, exploration, and imaginative expression in a pleasant, supportive atmosphere. Each child's work should be unique and recognizably different from another's. These process goals are best reached through traditional preschool techniques such as painting at an easel, finger painting, and rolling and molding clay.

The art experiences suggested in the *Library* are tied to particular curriculum topics. In this sense, the art activities are limited in their potential for pure, creative experience because they have been suggested as ways to reinforce certain ideas for the children. Keeping in mind that any activity described in this book is meant to be only *one* experience in a whole week of related activities, you must be certain to provide the children with plenty of pure art activities at other times. Opportunities for exploring color, line, and form and for discovering the effects of various media on different surfaces in an open-ended fashion will allow each child to make a personal statement with art.

Exposure to beautiful works of art can enhance the classroom environment. A number of activities include suggestions for obtaining inexpensive, high-quality color reproductions from the National Gallery of Art. These have special appeal for young children, such as the work of Renoir and Matisse.

Music. The goals of the music experiences are to develop appreciation, participation, and responsiveness; musical competencies such as listening, performance, rhythm, and creativity; and musical concepts such as pitch, volume, and contrasts. Many recorded songs are suggested along with new original music specifically designed for this curriculum. In addition, certain classical pieces that provide stimulating background music and exposure to the works of great composers are recommended.

Math. The math activities attempt to reflect the needs of the preoperational child, ages two to seven. Opportunities are presented that allow children to learn through direct experiences such as sorting, comparing, and ordering. Playful lessons develop skills in rote counting, numeral recognition, and sets. Again, duplicated sheets are not utilized in any of the math activities because they are a semiconcrete rather than a concrete vehicle for learning.

Thinking and Gross Motor Games. The thinking games motivate children to develop cognitive skills within a play situation. When involved in a thinking game, children are learning to identify, classify, and apply skills.

Gross motor games contribute to positive physical and mental health by strengthening muscles and helping to free children from tension. Social development is aided when the children cooperate and learn the positions of leader and follower. Finally, self-concepts are enhanced as youngsters acquire motor skills and feelings of success and enjoyment.

A Complete Preschool Development Plan consisting of the three Checklists is included at the end of each book. This Plan displays the developmental skills progression for two-, three-, and four-year-olds, giving you a clear picture of the prekindergarten skills children can be expected to develop. While educators know that learning is uneven (that is, a child who is three may not necessarily demonstrate all the three-year-old skills), the Plan gives you an overall idea of how normal development progresses and a place to start in assessing children's development. It also serves as a visual presentation of the cognitive theory that ideas grow from concrete to abstract and from simple to complex as the child learns and grows.

The three books in the *Library* can be used independently or simultaneously by a school that has classes for two-, three-, and four-year-olds. The children can study the same topics but in ways that are of interest to and appropriate for their level of growth. This exciting concept can mobilize a school and encourage total involvement of students, teachers, and parents in learning—all working together to help the children develop and grow to their fullest potential.

Anthony J. Coletta
Kathleen Coletta

CONTENTS

LEARNING ABOUT OURSELVES AND OTHERS

○ Getting to Know One Another

○ Self-Concept

○ Friends and School

Weekly Subtheme: Getting to Know One Another

III–1 NAME TAG NECKLACE

Subject Area: Art

Concepts/Skills: Verbally identifies letters in first name
Shows an interest in the printed name
Follows simple directions

Objectives: The children will help construct name tags and gain awareness of their printed names.

Materials:
- Pre-cut shapes (basic geometric shapes, animals, etc.) from manila or white heavy construction paper
- 36″ length of heavy red, yellow, or blue yarn for each child
- Watercolors
- Brushes
- Marker
- Hole puncher
- Clear self-stick vinyl (optional)
- Paper reinforcers (optional)

Procedure:

1. Introduce the children to the idea of name tags representing each one's name.
2. Allow the children time to select the pre-cut shapes (three samples are shown here) they want to use as name tags. Then let them choose watercolors to paint their nametags.

3. When the shapes are dry, ask each child his or her name and print it on the name tag as the child watches.
4. Punch a hole or two in the shape. (To add strength, you might want to cover the name tag with vinyl or use paper reinforcers over the holes before stringing.) Help the child thread the yarn through the hole and then tie the ends together yourself.
5. Let the children wear the necklaces after saying their names and pointing to the letters on the shapes.

Variations/Ways to Extend:

- Use the same shape of the name tag for the child's cubby hole, coat hook, and other personal places.
- For a daily opening activity, hang a pegboard with hooks where name tags can be hung individually. As the children enter the classroom, direct them to the pegboard to identify and remove their name tag necklaces and wear them each day for awhile. Call attention to their name tags and their names throughout the day by asking such questions as "Can you find something that matches Joey's red name tag?"

III–2 I DO!

Subject Area: Music

Concepts/Skills: Verbalizes songs
Recalls information previously taught
Touches and names parts of the body

Objective: The children will sing a song that will help them to get to know one another's name.

Materials:
- Words and music to the song
- Name tag for each child

Procedure:

1. Make a name tag for each child in your group (or use those made in Activity III–1).
2. Teach the song "I Do!" to the children and let them sing along as a group. Then sing the song to individual children, asking the particular child to sing the "I do, I do, I do" refrain. For examples, "Timmy, if you have two (blue, green, brown) eyes, say, 'I do.' ".
3. Continue around the group, verbalizing the names to reinforce them for the children.

Variations/Ways to Extend:

- Put the word *Me* in the center of a bulletin board and tape instant photos of all the children around it. Label each picture with the child's name. Then prepare a set of cards that the children may use to match configurations of the letters. Tell the children they may match their own name card to the label on the picture or practice with their friends' name cards and labels.
- Place a "magic mirror" in a box. Ask each child to look inside to see a very special, important person.

I Do

Words and Music by **BOB MESSANO**
Arranged by John Sheehan

© 1986 by The Center for Applied Research in Education, Inc.

Copyright 1984 Bob Messano

2. If you have a nose, say, "I Do!"
   If you have a nose, say, "I Do!"
   If you have a nose—
   Some fingers and some toes,
   Say "I Do! I Do! I Do!"

3. If you have two feet, say, "I Do!"
   If you have two feet, say, "I Do!"
   If you have two feet
   Tell everybody you meet—
   Say "I Do! I Do! I Do!"

4. If you have a head, say, "I Do!"
   If you have a head, say, "I Do!"
   If you have a head—
   To lay in your bed,
   Say "I Do! I Do! I Do!"

III–3   WHAT CAN YOU DO?

Subject Area: Creative Dramatics and Movement

Concepts/Skills: Speaks in sentences of six or more words
Participates verbally and nonverbally in imaginative play

Objectives: The children will introduce themselves to a puppet and play an imaginative game.

Materials: • Puppet (any puppet character with a name)
• Paper bag

Procedure:

1. Place the paper bag over the puppet and say to the children, "We have a special visitor today, someone who is very shy and does not want to come out of this paper bag." Encourage the children to ask the puppet to meet them.
2. Show the puppet and demonstrate the proper way to introduce oneself. Say, "Hello, [name of puppet]. My name is [your name]." Hold the puppet in front of each child and ask for an introduction, allowing everyone to participate.
3. Now play a game called "What Can You Do?" Introduce a child and then whisper a pretend idea for body movement (tying shoes, cutting with scissors, climbing a ladder, skipping, hopping, painting, etc.) into the child's ear. Ask the puppet and the other children to guess what the child is doing.

Variation/Way to Extend:

• Play a record to which the children will have fun moving. One such song is "Funky Penguin" from Hap Palmer's album *Movin'* (available from Educational Activities, Inc., Box 392, Freeport, NY 11520). Ask the children to move creatively to the music. Then when the music stops, ask them to hold hands with another child and take turns introducing themselves.

III–4 MY FRIEND

Subject Area: Art

Concepts/Skills: Dictates own experience stories
Works and plays cooperatively with other children

Objectives: The children will draw pictures of their friends, dictate descriptions of them, and look at friendship books.

Materials:
- Pre-cut friendship book for each child (see pattern)
- Drawing paper
- Crayons
- Marker
- Book

Procedure:

1. Read a book on friendship, such as *Ira Sleeps Over* by Bernard Waber (Boston: Houghton-Mifflin, 1975). Discuss with the children the book and the idea of friendship.
2. Ask the children to draw pictures of their friends on drawing paper.
3. As the children describe their friends' finished drawings, write down in their friendship books what they say.

Variation/Way to Extend:

- Set up a "My Friend" area in the room and have several friendship books available for the children to add drawings and statements as they get to know one another. Send these books home occasionally so that the children can inform their parents about their new friends.

© 1986 by The Center for Applied Research in Education, Inc.

FRIENDSHIP

III–5   WHAT I LIKE ABOUT MYSELF

Subject Area: Social Studies

Concepts/Skills: Feels good about self
Verbalizes a song
Makes relevant contribution in small group discussion

Objectives: The children will recall what they like best about themselves and sing a song.

Materials:
- Words to "It's Me"
- Drawing Paper
- Crayons
- Scissors
- Marker
- Oaktag
- Paste

Procedure:

1. Introduce the following song entitled "It's Me" to the children. Sing it to the tune of "Where is Thumbkin?" and repeat the words to help the children learn it. You might also let the children introduce themselves to one another.

   I am special, I am special.
   Turn around, you will see
   Someone really special, someone really special.
   Yes, it's me; yes, it's me.

2. Ask the children to name something they like about themselves (facial features, clothes, homes, family members, etc.) and to draw a little picture of it.

3. Help the children to cut out these pictures and then make a chart of the results.

	👀	👄	😊	hair	✋	🏠
Pat				hair		
Carol		👄			✋	
Mark			😊			
Paul	👀					🏠

Variation/Way to Extend:
- Read *Andy: That's My Name* by Tomie De Paola (Englewood Cliffs, NJ: Prentice-Hall, 1973).

Weekly Subtheme: Self-Concept

III–6 THE "ME" DOLL

Subject Area: Art

Concepts/Skills: Touches and names parts of the body
Controls brush and paint
Uses scissors with control

Objective: The children will construct life-size images of themselves.

Materials:
- Roll of wide paper
- Paints
- Brushes
- Newspapers
- Side from a refrigerator-size cardboard box
- Scissors
- Stapler

Procedure:

1. Ask each child to lie on the paper and then trace around the child. Then have the child name the parts of his or her body on the life-size drawing.
2. Have the children paint in facial features, clothing, and hair.
3. Lay the dried painting on the large piece of cardboard. Lay a second sheet of paper beneath the painting and help the child cut out the two sheets together around the body outline.
4. Staple halfway up the two sheets and carefully stuff with newspaper, continuing until the life-size doll is finished.

Variations/Ways to Extend:

- Make these dolls more elaborate by using yarn to paste on as hair. You might even dress the figures in children's clothing.
- Play the recording "You Look So Sweet" by Ella Jenkins from the album *Seasons for Singing* (Folkways Records, 632 Broadway, New York, NY 10012).

III–7 FINGERPRINT FLOWERS AND BUTTERFLIES

Concepts/Skills: Observes objects closely
Proposes alternative ways of doing something
Acts out a rhyme as the teacher recites

Objectives: The children will take their own fingerprints and create drawings from them.

Materials:
- Book
- Index cards
- Ink pad
- Felt-tip pens
- Magnifying glasses

Procedure:

1. Read the book *My Hands* by Aliki (New York: Harper & Row, 1962) and then begin a discussion about hands. Teach the children the saying "Five on one hand, ten on two hands (clap)."
2. Have the children examine their own hands and fingers and those of their classmates with a magnifying glass.
3. Ask the children to put each finger of one hand on the ink pad and make their prints on an index card. Ask them how these prints could be turned into flowers, animals, or other things they are familiar with. For example, the children could envision their prints as the center of a flower and draw on the petals, or they can draw wings around their prints and add a body in the center to form butterflies.

4. Compare the prints and help the children learn that no two people have the same prints. Label each child's prints and keep them in a file box where they can look up their prints later.
5. Now recite the following rhyme as the children act it out:

   Reach for the ceiling, touch the floor,
   Stand up again, let's do more.
   Touch your head, then your knees,
   Wiggle your nose, touch your shoulders.
   Reach for the ceiling, touch the floor,
   That's all now, there won't be more.

Variations/Ways to Extend:

- Invite parents to volunteer their fingerprints to add to the display area.
- Make prints from a cat, two dogs of different sizes, a guinea pig, and other animals. Let the children compare these prints and talk about likenesses and differences.

III–8 LET'S COUNT

Subject Area: Math

Concepts/Skills: Counts from one to ten
Verbalizes a fingerplay

Objectives: The children will develop their skills in counting and in recognizing left and right.

Materials: • Words to the fingerplay
• Colored string

Procedure:

1. Teach the children the following number fingerplay. Show them how to hold up their fingers one at a time as they are counted:

   One, two, three, four, five,
   One day I caught a fish alive.
   Six, seven, eight, nine, ten,
   Then I let it go again.
   Why did you let it go?
   Because it bit my finger so.
   Which finger did it bite?
   The pinky finger on the right.

2. Ask each child to raise the right hand and then tie a colored string around the right wrist. Refer to right and left throughout the day and repeat from time to time throughout the day and throughout the year for reinforcement of the concept.

Variations/Ways to Extend:

- Read *Numbers* by John J. Reiss (Scarsdale, NY: Bradbury Press, 1971).
- Reinforce the counting exercise by using felt cutouts on a flannelboard to show how each number is one more than the preceding number.
- Hide "treasures" around the room and let all the children hunt around to find them. When all have been found, ask the children to line them up on a table and count them.

III–9   I CAN DO IT MYSELF

Subject Area: Language Arts

Concepts/Skills: Listens to stories
Develops fine motor and eye–hand coordination
Feels good about self

Objectives: The children will practice such self-help tasks as buttoning, zippering, snapping, and tying laces.

Materials:
- Clothes and shoes
- Book
- Markers
- Oaktag
- Lacing and sewing cards (optional)
- Group photo
- Scissors
- Paste
- Pre-made pictures

Procedure:

1. Read *Growing Up* by Jean Fritz (Eau Claire, WI: Hale, 1956).
2. Instruct those children who need help in managing buttons, snaps, and zippers. If necessary, have a special lesson on tying shoes. Explain it this way: Take one lace and make a loop (bunny ear). Make a loop with the other lace (two loops) and make an *X* with the two bunny ears. One ear comes through the hole. Pull tightly. (You might also have the children practice with lacing and sewing cards.)
3. For the chart, take a group photo of the children and cut it apart so that you have an image of each child to glue down the left side of the oaktag. Then use pre-made small pictures to glue on the chart horizontally as the children master various skills. (**Note:** This chart accentuates what the children have been able to achieve rather than pointing up what they have yet to master.) Be sure each child has at least one little picture after his or her name.

	I Can Do It Myself!			
Bill				
Jen	◌ ◉			
Gail		∿∿⋙		
Tim				
Pam			👟	
Kris		⊛ ⊛		

(Use photos here)

Variation/Way to Extend:

- Talk about how enjoyable it is to be self-reliant. Explain patience and that it takes time to learn new skills.

III-10 FOUR CLUES

Subject Area: Thinking Games

Concepts/Skills: Verbalizes address, age, birthday, and phone number
Listens to directions for games and activities

Objective: The children will participate in a game in which they have to listen carefully for information that pertains to themselves.

Material: • Class list

Procedure:

1. Explain to the children that they are going to play a game in which listening is very important. Say a child's address, age, birthday, and phone number aloud to the group and see if the particular child recognizes the information given as his or her own.
2. As each child is accounted for in the game, have that child repeat what was heard; that is, say his or her own address, age, birthday, phone number, and full name. (**Note:** If your group is large, do this activity in several sittings.)

Variation/Way to Extend:

• If approved in your school, compile and duplicate this information and make "Our Superstars" booklets to be sent home as class directories for parents and children.

III-11 MY SCHOOL

Subject Area: Art

Concepts/Skills: Asks an increasing number of questions
Recalls information previously taught
Represents thoughts in pictures

Objectives: The children will recall and draw a person or object they observed on their walking tour.

Materials:
- Construction paper
- Crayons
- Glue
- Large sheet of oaktag
- Marker

Procedure:

1. Draw a large building and put the name of your school or center on it. Then take a walking tour to see other rooms, meet other staff members, and observe the layout and equipment. Encourage the children to ask questions. Ask them to repeat the names of the director, nurse, teachers, bus driver, and others.

2. Upon return to the classroom, have the children draw and color a small picture of something or someone they saw around the school. Glue these to the large school picture and display at the children's eye-level.

Variations/Ways to Extend:

- Talk with the children about the location of the school. Ask such questions as "What is the name of this street?" and "How do you travel to school?"
- Take photos of the people, rooms, and equipment around the center and put them up as a wall display at the children's eye-level. Ask the children to share their reactions to the photos. Write down these comments on small cards and attach them next to the photos.

Weekly Subtheme: Friends and School

III–12   SKIP TAG

Subject Area: Gross Motor Games

Concepts/Skills: Listens to directions for a game
Develops gross motor movement of skipping

Objective: The children will learn to play a skipping game.

Materials: • Large open area
• Music (optional)

Procedure:

1. Encourage the children to practice skipping while singing "Skip to My Lou."
2. Now ask the children to hold hands, make a circle, and drop hands. Have them hold both hands out in front. Pick one child to skip around inside the circle and "tag" the hands of the child of his or her choice. Tell the tagged child to skip around the circle in the opposite direction from the first child and to shake hands with the other child when they meet. Have the first child return to his or her place; and ask the second child to continue to skip around and tag someone else.
3. Continue until all the children have participated. Play suitable music if you like.

Variation/Way to Extend:

• Play "Hello Song" from the children's television show "The Magic Garden." It is recorded on *Paula and Carole in the Magic Garden*, available from CAP Publications, Inc., Box 101, Scarsdale, NY 10583.

III–13 HOW TALL ARE WE?

Subject Area: Math

Concepts/Skills: Compares size differences
Understands "taller" and "shorter"

Objective: The children will compare their heights.

Materials:
- Different colors of construction paper
- Tape
- Scissors
- Measuring tape
- Marker

Procedure:

1. Measure each child's height. Cut strips of colored construction paper to accurately represent each measurement and tape these strips to a wall.

2. Write each child's name and height in inches on separate pieces of paper and tape them onto the wall at the top and along the side of each colored strip as shown below. When completed, assist the children in comparing heights, such as "Melissa is taller than Michael."

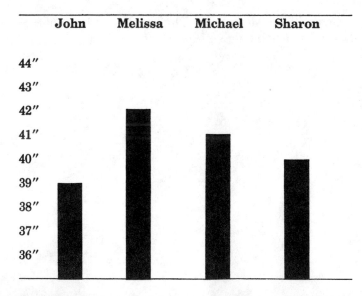

3. Periodically throughout the year, measure the children and add paper strips to reflect their growth.

Variation/Way to Extend:

- Create a separate graph for measuring the weights of the children. After recording their weights (use a bathroom scale), create a bar graph. Again, assist the children in comparing differences in weight. (**Note:** Be sure to carry out this activity in a way that is fun and in no way judgmental.)

III–14 ON THE ROAD TO SCHOOL

Subject Area: Science

Concepts/Skills: Shows an increasing curiosity and sense of adventure
Pays attention and concentrates on a task

Objectives: The children will construct traffic lights and learn a safety poem.

Materials:
- Words to the poem
- Pre-cut red, yellow, and green circles
- Paper bag for each child
- Pictures
- Paste

Procedure:

1. Show pictures and discuss with the children the methods of transportation they use to get to school. Talk about safety and then teach the following safety poem:

   Red says STOP,
   Green says GO,
   Yellow says BE CAREFUL, I'm changing now you know.
   Red says STOP,
   Green says GO,
   Yellow says WAIT, you'd better go slow!
   When I reach a crossing place,
   I look both ways by turning my face,
   I walk, not run, across the street
   And use my head to guide my feet.

2. Have the children paste the red, yellow, and green circles on the paper bags. Tell the children that they can put their arms in the bags and hold them up to play "traffic light."

Variations/Ways to Extend:

- Begin a discussion about what would happen without traffic lights. Let the children dramatize the situation.
- Listen to "Stop, Look and Listen" on Hap Palmer's *Learning Basic Skills Through Music—Health and Safety*, available from Educational Activities, Inc., Box 392, Freeport, NY 11520.

III-15 NEIGHBORS IN SCHOOL

Subject Area: Music

Concepts/Skills: Participates and responds with pleasure
Marches in time with music

Objectives: The children will sing together, play rhythm instruments, and march to a song.

Materials:
- Record album
- Record player
- Rhythm instruments

Procedure:

1. Introduce the album *Won't You Be My Neighbor?* by Fred Rogers (Columbia Records, #CC24516). As many children will probably be familiar with Mr. Rogers' theme song, "Won't You Be My Neighbor?" let them sing this song together. (If this album is not available, choose another with the theme of friendship.)

2. Select another song on the album to which the children can move and march. Ask one child to distribute five rhythm instruments to five different children to reinforce one-to-one correspondence as well as counting. Have another child distribute five more instruments. Then ask the children to form a line and march in a parade, playing the rhythm instruments to accompany the music.

Variation/Way to Extend:

- Hang a variety of wind chimes on a nearby tree for the children to listen to when they are playing outside. Make one type by stringing small seashells on fishline and threading the ends through a wicker trivet. Attach another length of fishline to the top and hang.

HARVEST TIME AND THE FARM

- ○ Colors
- ○ Foods
- ○ Farm and Farm Animals
- ○ Halloween

III-16 HAND-PRINTED LEAVES

Subject Area: Art

Concepts/Skills: Uses crayon with control
Points to and names colors

Objective: The children will create colorful fall pictures.

Materials:
- White paper
- Brown crayons
- Dried grass, dried flowers, and twigs
- Water
- Paper towels
- Glue
- Fall-colored tempera paints

Procedure:

1. Have the children draw tree trunks by holding an unwrapped brown crayon sideways and using downward strokes. Tell the children to add branches by making a few upward strokes that fan out from the top of the trunk.
2. Now help the children dip each hand, palm down, into separate tempera paints and press their palms on paper in different positions. Help the children wash their hands if they want to use two other colors. Encourage the children to identify the colors and explain that the effect is similar to that of multi-colored leaves on the trees.
3. Let the children fill in the background by gluing dried grass, dried flowers, and twigs onto the paper.

Variation/Way to Extend:

- Read *What Is the Color of the Wide, Wide World?* by Margaret Friskey (Chicago: Childrens Press, 1973).

III-17 WAX PAPER TRANSLUCENTS

Subject Areas: Science and Art

Concepts/Skills: Uses scissors with control
Explores new materials
Observes objects closely

Objective: The children will create translucent collages from fall leaf shapes.

Materials:
- Colored tissue paper
- Pencils
- Scissors
- Wax paper
- Pre-cut cardboard leaf patterns
- Newspapers
- Food warming tray
- Rolling pin
- Hole puncher
- String

Procedure:

1. Help the children trace leaf shapes onto colored tissue paper and carefully cut them out.
2. Arrange the paper leaves between two sheets of wax paper. Have the children seal the papers together by placing them on a newspaper-covered food warming tray and rubbing firmly across the wax paper with a rolling pin. (**Caution:** Be sure the children do this only under teacher supervision.)
3. Punch a hole near the top center of the sealed collage, place a length of string through it, and hang it in front of a sunny window.

Variations/Ways to Extend:

- Staple or tape string to the sealed paper in order to suspend it from the ceiling.
- Try pressing real autumn leaves, feathers, colored thread, glitter, and/or tiny flowers between the wax paper.
- Read *The House of Four Seasons* by Roger Duvoisin (New York: Lothrop, 1956).

III–18   COLOR DAY

Subject Area: Thinking Games

Concept/Skill: Points to and names colors

Objective: The children will match basic colors.

Materials: • Pre-cut cartoon characters, each in a different color
   • Safety pins

Procedure:

1. Be sure that each cartoon character is cut from different-colored construction paper, such as a yellow bird and a green dog.
2. Pin the characters onto the children's clothing and ask them to find objects in the room that are the same color as their particular character.

Variation/Way to Extend:

• Read *Caps for Sale* by Esphyr Slobodkina (Reading, MA: Addison-Wesley, 1947).

III-19   MY COLOR BOOK

Subject Area: Language Arts

Concepts/Skills: Reproduces a circle
Uses a crayon with control
Points to and names colors

Objective: The children will construct a color book.

Materials: • Six sheets of white drawing paper folded into four squares for each child
• Crayons
• Stapler

Procedure:

1. Give each child one folded sheet at a time to color objects for a color page. Say, "Draw four yellow objects [very simple drawings, circles, grass, balls, face, sun], one in each square of the paper."
2. Have the children do this for five other pages of red, blue, green, purple, and orange objects.
3. Then staple the books together and display on a color table.

Variations/Ways to Extend:

• At another time, add pages for black, white, and brown.
• Cut out paper fish of the colors mentioned under "Procedure" and attach paper clips to them. Allow the children to fish using wooden dowels with string and magnets attached.

III–20   COLOR CARD GAME

Subject Area: Math

Concepts/Skills: Counts from one to six
Points to and names colors

Objective: The children will pair matching color cards.

Material: • Teacher-made deck of twenty-four color cards.

Procedure:

1. Cut out four cards each in the six basic colors (red, orange, green, blue, yellow, and violet). Paste these colored paper rectangles onto white tagboard cards.

2. Deal each of four children a hand of six color cards and encourage them to count the six cards.
3. Have the children take turns asking one another for a specific color to make a pair. Tell the children to lay down any matched pairs.
4. Continue until all the cards are used.

Variation/Way to Extend:

• During the week, read excerpts from *Hailstones & Halibut Bones* by Mary O'Neill (New York: Doubleday, no date). It is a book of poetry about colors.

III-21   SNACK PLATE

Subject Area: Nutrition and Foods Experience

Concept/Skill: Describes foods by taste (sweet, sour, salty)

Objective: The children will describe the taste of foods from the four food groups.

Materials: • Paper plates
• Foods from basic four food groups

Procedure:

1. Prepare a snack plate of small bite-sized pieces of food chosen from the four food groups. Examples are:

   Fruit and Vegetable—slices of apple, orange, banana; pieces of carrot, celery, cauliflower, pickle
   Bread and Cereal—small crackers; pieces of whole grain bread
   Milk and Cheese—small pieces of cheeses; cup of milk
   Protein—slices of hard-boiled egg; small pieces of cooked ham or beef

   Include at least one representative food from each group.

2. As the children taste each snack, mention the corresponding food group. Encourage the children to describe the food as sweet, sour, or salty.

Variations/Ways to Extend:

• Play food riddles with the children. Give clues about a food and ask the children to guess what it is.
• Obtain an 11″ × 14″ art reproduction of "Still Life with Apples and Peaches" by Paul Cézanne from the National Gallery of Art, Publications Service, Washington, DC 20565. Be sure to write for a catalog and prices.

III–22 FARM MARKET STAND

Subject Area: Social Studies

Concepts/Skills: Demonstrates accurate sense of smell, taste, and touch
Reproduces a simple pattern of different items from memory

Objective: The children will go on a field trip to a farm market.

Materials:
- Trip arrangements
- Pre-cut fall food name tags
- Safety pins
- Knife and peeler
- Money to purchase items
- Felt-backed pictures
- Flannelboard

Procedure:

1. Arrange for a class trip to a farm, farm market, or grocery store produce section. Discuss with the children the name tags and the fruits and vegetables they represent. Tell the children that when they get to the market, they are to see if they can find the fruit or vegetable that matches the one on their name tag. Remind the children that the actual item may be larger (or smaller) than on the name tag.

2. At the market, buy at least one of each of the name tag items and let the children help you weigh them, purchase them, and carry them back to school.
3. In the classroom, have the children examine their purchases, feel them, smell them, and taste any that can be eaten raw. Talk about the color and texture of each.
4. After the children have examined and tasted the foods, place three pictures of food items, such as corn, bread, and milk, on the flannelboard and ask the children to look at them for several seconds. Remove the pictures and ask a child to put them back up in order. Repeat the procedure with other children and other food pictures.

Variations/Ways to Extend:

- Cook the vegetables and compare them with the raw ones. Have the children notice any difference in color.
- Write a simple experience story about the trip to the market. Let each child tell something and include the child's name in the story, such as "Mark found orange pumpkins at the market."
- If corn is one of the vegetables, make popcorn and show the children the kernels.
- Play "grocery store" with the children. Bring in empty cartons and cans and provide a toy cash register, play money, and shopping bags for the children to use in dramatic play.

III-23   VEGETABLE DYEING

Subject Area: Art

Concepts/Skills: Predicts outcome of events
Dictates experience story

Objective: The children will create colored cloth by boiling fruits and vegetables for color.

Materials:
- Pieces of white cloth
- Onion skins
- Blackberries (or blueberries)
- Beets
- Spinach leaves
- Four containers
- Pot
- Heat source

Procedure:

1. Boil water. (**Caution:** Be sure the children stay away from the heat source.) Place a different fruit or vegetable in each container, add the boiling water, and allow to cool.
2. Along with the children, carefully dip pieces of white cloth into each solution. As the cloth is lowered into the containers, ask the children to guess what color the cloth will turn.
3. After the dyeing process is finished, have the children compare their predictions with the results observed:

   Onion skins—yellow or red
   Blackberries (or blueberries)—blue
   Beets—red or violet
   Spinach leaves—green

4. Using the children's own words, write an experience chart of the activity.

Variations/Ways to Extend:

- Read *Blueberries for Sal* by Robert McCloskey (New York: Viking, 1948).
- Read the poem "Raw Carrots" by Valerie Worth, found in her book of poetry entitled *Small Poems* (New York: Farrar, Straus & Giroux, 1975).

III-24 POTATO HEAD

Subject Area: Science

Concepts/Skills: Observes objects closely
Understands that plants need water, light, warmth, and air to live

Objectives: The children will grow "grass hair" from seed and create a potato head.

Materials:
- Potato for each child
- Paper towels
- Grass seed
- Knife
- Cloves
- Glass of water for each child
- Toothpicks

Procedure:

1. Stand each potato on end and slice off the top. Have the children place a wet piece of paper towel over the cut portion of the potato.
2. Insert three toothpicks into each potato, stand it in a glass of water, and place each one on a windowsill. Have the children sprinkle the wet paper towel with grass seed.
3. Ask the children to keep the paper towel moist every day. Tell them that the seeds will soon sprout and the "potato head" will grow "green hair." Let the children use cloves to add eyes, a nose, and a mouth to their potato head.

Variation/Way to Extend:

- Let the children observe that potatoes, too, started from seeds. Show them the parts of a potato (eye, sprout, root, vine).

III–25   PEANUT BUTTER BALLS

Subject Area: Nutrition and Foods Experience

Concept/Skill: Develops fine motor movements of measuring and rolling

Objectives: The children will participate in making peanut butter and follow a recipe for the peanut butter snack.

Materials:
- 1 cup peanuts
- 1½ tablespoons oil
- Salt
- 15 ounces graham crackers
- 2 tablespoons corn syrup
- 2 tablespoons milk
- 4 tablespoons butter
- 2 tablespoons vanilla
- Blender
- Self-closing plastic bag
- Rolling pin
- Measuring utensils
- Mixing bowls

Procedure:

1. Tell the children that peanuts are high in protein, which helps give us muscle and energy. Also tell the children that they are going to make their own peanut butter for a snack treat.
2. Put the oil in a blender and gradually add the peanuts. Sprinkle with a little salt and blend well. Set aside.
3. To make the peanut butter balls, place the graham crackers in the plastic bag and let the children crush them with the rolling pin. Cream the butter and add the corn syrup, milk, vanilla, and peanut butter. Ask a child to add one cup of the graham cracker crumbs. Let the children mix the ingredients thoroughly and then roll into 1″ balls. Have the children roll the balls in the remaining crumbs.
4. Enjoy the peanut butter balls with milk or juice at snack time.

Variation/Way to Extend:

- Listen to the song "Kinds of Food" on Hap Palmer's *Learning Basic Skills Through Music—Vocabulary*, available from Educational Activities, Inc., Box 392, Freeport, NY 11520.

III-26   THE FARMER SCRAPBOOK

Subject Area: Science

Concepts/Skills: Makes a simple comparison of pictures in terms of difference
Compares size differences
Observes pictures closely

Objective: The children will create a farm scrapbook.

Materials: • Pictures
• Scrapbook
• Glue
• Marker

Procedure:

1. Collect pictures about farms and farm animals (cows, pigs, rabbits, horses, ducks, chicks, hens, roosters, sheep, goats, and turkeys). Discuss with the children characteristics of each animal and have the children compare them (large/small, number of legs, mouth/beak, skin/feathers/hair, walk/fly/swim, sounds, provide food or clothing, work for people).

2. Have the children paste each picture on a page in the scrapbook and let them dictate a few words about what they have learned about each one.

Variations/Ways to Extend:

• Read the Caldecott Medal winner *Make Way for Ducklings* by Robert McCloskey (New York: Viking, 1941).

• Make butter from cream by placing a small amount of room-temperature heavy cream into a baby food jar and shaking it until butter forms. Let the children watch the cream separate and become butter. Point out the curds (lumps) and the whey (watery part) and recite "Little Miss Muffet."

• Try an old-fashioned way of coloring the butter. Shred raw carrots until fine. Place the shreds in cheesecloth and squeeze out the orange-colored juice into the butter. Then mix to the desired yellow color.

III–27   FARM RIDDLES

Subject Area: Language Arts

Concepts/Skills: Orally labels pictures
Recalls information previously taught

Objective: The children will apply their knowledge of farm animals by answering questions and riddles.

Material: • Pictures

Procedure:

1. Display pictures of farm animals and ask the children questions about the animals. Have them respond verbally and/or by pointing to the appropriate picture. For example, say, "Pick out an animal that has feathers." (duck, turkey, hen) "What animal says 'oink, oink'?" (pig) "Point to an animal with a mane." (horse) "Which animal says 'gobble, gobble'?" (turkey)

2. Ask the children to answer these farm riddles:

   I am yellow.
   I like grain.
   My mother's a hen.
   Who am I? (a chick)

   Your scarf came from my wool.
   I am usually white.
   My daddy is a ram.
   Who am I? (a lamb)

   I give you milk.
   I like to eat grass.
   My baby is a calf.
   Who am I? (a cow)

   I have long legs.
   I eat oats and hay.
   My son is a colt.
   Who am I? (a horse)

Variations/Ways to Extend:

• Read *The Little Farm* by Lois Lenski (New York: McKay, 1942).
• Obtain an 11″ × 14″ art reproduction of "Child in a Straw Hat" (#2892) by Mary Cassatt from the National Gallery of Art, Publications Service, Washington, DC 20565. Be sure to write for a catalog and prices.

III–28   "TALKIN' TO AN OWL" BLUES

Subject Area: Music

Concepts/Skills: Verbalizes a song
Participates with pleasure

Objective: The children will participate in learning a song about animal sounds.

Material: • Words and music to the song

Procedure:

1. Introduce the song "Talkin' to an Owl Blues" and teach the words to the children.
2. Allow the children to sing along as a group.

Variation/Way to Extend:

• Read *Farm Counting Book* by Jane Miller (Englewood Cliffs, NJ: Prentice-Hall, 1983).

Talkin' to an Owl Blues

Words and Music by **BOB MESSANO**
Arranged by John Sheehan

© 1986 by The Center for Applied Research in Education, Inc.

Copyright 1984 Bob Messano

© 1986 by The Center for Applied Research in Education, Inc.

2. Then I met a cow, out in the field,
   I said, "Hey, Mrs. Cow, how do you feel?"
   She said, "Moo! . . ."

3. I said to the rooster, "How do you do?"
   He looked at me and said, "Cockle-doodle-doo!"
   He said, "Cockle-doodle-doo! . . ."

4. Granny was afraid, because she saw a rat,
   She said, "Where's my old farm cat?"
   He said, "Mew! . . ."

Weekly Subtheme: Farm and Farm Animals

III-29 FARM MOBILE

Subject Area: Art

Concepts/Skills: Explores
Uses crayon with control

Objective: The children will construct a mobile of farm animals.

Materials:
- Pre-cut farm animal shapes
- String
- Dowels
- Glue
- Crayons
- Feathers
- Yarn
- Scissors

Procedure:

1. Cut the string into different lengths and tie to the dowels.
2. Ask the children to select a few animal shapes and color them. Then have the children paste on feathers and yarn for texture.
3. Glue the animal shapes onto the strings to create a mobile and hang the mobiles from the ceiling or doorway.

Variations/Ways to Extend:

- Read *A Farmer's Alphabet* by Mary Azarian (Boston: David R. Godine, 1981).
- Make a tasting table of foods that come from cows: milk, buttermilk, cheese, whipped cream, ice cream, butter, yogurt, sour cream, cottage cheese, and beef products. Let the children experience the various foods.

Weekly Subtheme: Farm and Farm Animals

III-30 HOW DID YOU GET THERE?

Subject Area: Creative Movement

Concepts/Skills: Moves body creatively upon teacher's command
Develops gross motor movements of running, galloping, hopping, and jumping

Objective: The children will react to auditory clues by demonstrating movement in a game.

Materials: • Large open space
• Another adult

Procedure:

1. Have the children start out on one side of an open area, with you with them. Ask another adult to be on the other side.
2. Say to the other adult, "Duck, duck, how did you get there?" Have the other adult shout back, "All of the ducks waddled." Upon hearing that statement, have the children waddle to where the other adult is standing.
3. Then have the adult with the children say, "Duck, duck, how did you get there?" You reply, "All of the ducks swam." The children must then "swim" back to you.
4. Continue with various other farm animals (horse—galloped, jumped; rabbit—ran, hopped; hen—scurried, clucked; etc.).

Variation/Way to Extend:

• Let the children build a farm yard from blocks and have them imitate various animals in their respective section of the farm (corral, henhouse, pen, pasture, pond). Ask the children to imitate sounds and characteristic movements of the animals as well as demonstrate their uses on a farm.

III-31   HALLOWEEN GAMES

Subject Area: Gross motor games

Concept/Skill: Moves creatively upon teacher's command

Objective: The children will play some games with Halloween as a focus.

Materials: • Large open area
• Orange balloons
• String

Procedure:

Introduce the children to the following games:

1. Play "Witch Says" in the same manner as "Simon Says."
2. Organize relay races with orange balloons tied to the children's ankles.
3. Have the children pretend that they are Halloween cats. Ask them to slowly and carefully use their opposite hand and leg to crawl.
4. Let the children be pumpkins. They all grow in a patch together, spread out on vines.

Variations/Ways to Extend:

• Listen to the song "Have a Good Time on Halloween" on Hap Palmer's album *Holiday Songs and Rhythms* (available from Educational Activities, Inc., Box 392, Freeport, NY 11520).
• For snack time, emphasize black and orange by having the children drink orange juice through "straws" made of licorice. Be sure to cut open the ends!

III–32   PUMPKIN SEEDS

Subject Area: Science

Concepts/Skills: Begins to develop a sense of taste
Understands that foods come from seeds

Objectives: The children will observe pumpkin seeds being cooked and then will enjoy eating them.

Materials:
- 2 cups pumpkin seeds
- 2 teaspoons salt
- 2 tablespoons melted butter
- Cookie sheet
- Oven
- Paper towels

Procedure:

1. Show the children the pumpkin seeds saved from a jack-o'-lantern. Explain to the children that these seeds can be planted, but that for today's activity, they will be dried and roasted.
2. Wash the seeds and dry them on paper towels. Then spread the seeds on a cookie sheet to thoroughly dry overnight.
3. The next day, combine the butter and salt and then toss with the seeds.
4. Bake on a cookie sheet for fifty minutes at 250° F, stirring every ten minutes until the seeds are lightly brown. (**Caution:** Be sure the children stay away from the heat.)
5. Serve the roasted seeds with juice for a snack. Be sure the children carefully chew the seeds.

Variations/Ways to Extend:

- Have the children make a seed collage by arranging the dried pumpkin seeds on dark paper and pasting them in place.
- Let the children help you dye the seeds different colors using food coloring and one teaspoon vinegar to each cup of water. Then ask the children to make seed pictures.
- Help the children make rattles or noisemakers by putting the dried seeds into empty boxes or round oatmeal containers.

III-33 WITCH PUPPET

Subject Area: Art

Concepts/Skills: Represents thoughts in pictures
Uses markers with control

Objective: The children will construct a Halloween paper bag puppet.

Materials:
- Pre-cut facial features
- Shiny black and silver paper
- Scissors
- Markers
- Black yarn
- White paper bag for each child
- Paste

Procedure:

1. Allow the children to choose facial features to make witches' faces on the paper bags. Help them to glue these in place.

2. Encourage the children to complete the witches' faces with drawn-in eyebrows, pupils, eyelashes, and teeth.
3. Help the children glue on a shiny hat and decorate with yarn for hair.

Variations/Ways to Extend:
- Use the witch puppets to role play safety rules for trick-or-treaters.
- Read *Trick or Treat* by Louis Slobodkin (New York: Macmillan, 1972).
- For background music this week, play "Witches' Dance" by MacDonald (RCA Basic Record Library).

Weekly Subtheme: Halloween

III-34 PUMPKIN COOKIES

Subject Area: Nutrition and Foods Experience

Concepts/Skills: Develops fine motor movements of mixing, pouring, and measuring
Understands fractions of ½ and ¼

Objective: The children will participate in a cooking experience.

Materials: (This recipe makes about three dozen cookies)
- ⅓ cup shortening
- ¾ cup sugar
- 1 egg
- 1 cup pumpkin
- 2¼ cups flour
- 4 teaspoons baking powder
- 1 teaspoon cinnamon
- ¼ teaspoon ginger
- ¼ teaspoon nutmeg
- ½ teaspoon salt
- ½ teaspoon vanilla
- 1 cup raisins (optional)
- ½ cup chopped nuts (optional)
- Baking utensils
- Oven

Procedure:

1. Acquaint the children with spices (see above ingredients) with which they may be unfamiliar.
2. To make the cookies, let the children help you cream the sugar and shortening. Add the egg, blend well, and then add the pumpkin. Sift together the dry ingredients and add to the egg mixture. If desired, fold in the raisins and nuts. Drop the batter by spoonfuls onto a greased cookie sheet and bake at 350° F for fifteen minutes. (**Caution:** Be sure the children stay away from the heat.)
3. Let the children enjoy the pumpkin cookies with milk or juice at snack time.

Variations/Ways to Extend:

- Read *Pumpkin Moonshine* by Tasha Tudor (New York: Walck, 1962).
- Bring in both powdered and whole spices, such as cinnamon, ginger, and nutmeg, and let the children compare the scents, shapes, textures, and tastes.

Weekly Subtheme: Halloween

III–35   HALLOWEEN NUMBERS

Subject Area: Math

Concepts/Skills: Recognizes and orders cardinal numerals from one to ten
Establishes one-to-one correspondence

Objective: The children will demonstrate correspondence between numerals and sets of Halloween shapes.

Materials: • Pre-cut felt numerals and shapes
• Flannelboard

Procedure:

1. Place the felt numerals in sequence on the flannelboard.
2. Ask the children to place the correct number of shapes under each, as shown in the illustration.

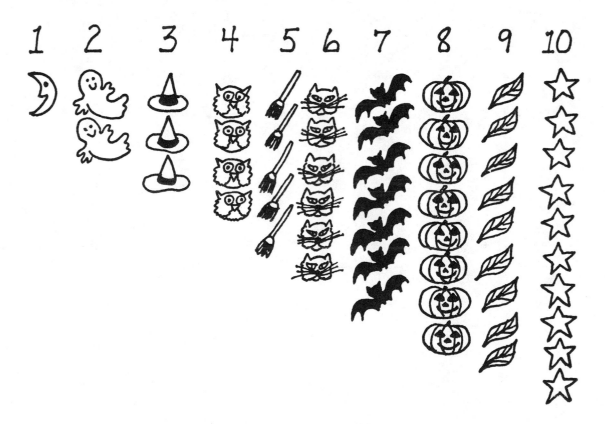

Variations/Ways to Extend:

- Use the felt materials in other ways. You might, for example, ask the children to sort the shapes; use the numerals to show two- and three-digit numbers; and use the shapes to show the results of adding one or more to a group or taking one or more away from a group.
- For an art experience, have the children drop splashes of orange and black paint onto a piece of paper. Ask the children to fold the paper in half to create double-image shapes and label them as witches, ghosts, and pumpkins.

HOME AND FAMILY

○ My Family

○ My Home and Neighborhood

○ American Indians

○ Thanksgiving

III-36   FAMILIES AT WORK AND AT PLAY

Subject Area: Social Studies

Concepts/Skills: Orally labels pictures and drawings

Develops fine motor movements of using crayons, brushes, and scissors with control

Represents thoughts in pictures

Understands that families share responsibilities of work and recreation

Objective: The children will draw, paint, or cut out pictures to make a class book about families.

Materials:
- Paper
- Scissors
- Crayons
- Glue
- Paints
- Brushes
- Magazines
- Stapler

Procedure:

1. Discuss with the children how families work together to make their homes clean and happy and how they also have fun together.
2. Ask the children to draw, paint, or cut from magazines pictures representing families in action. Label "Families at Work" those pages showing male and female workers in various household jobs. Label "Families at Play" those pages showing people picnicking, vacationing, swimming, dancing, or engaging in similar activities.
3. Help the children to put the pages together to form a class book.

Variation/Way to Extend:

- Read *What Mary Jo Shared* by Janice M. Udry (New York: Scholastic, 1970). Ask the children to tell about the most important part of the story. Were they surprised?

III-37 BABY IN A CRADLE

Subject Area: Art

Concepts/Skills: Uses brush and paint with control
Participates verbally or nonverbally in imaginative play

Objective: The children will construct a cradle, blanket, and baby doll.

Materials:
- Oatmeal carton for each child
- Tempera paints
- Brushes
- Felt-tip pens
- Utility knife
- Paste
- Scraps of yarn and fabric
- Clothespins
- Scissors

Procedure:

1. Cut the oatmeal cartons in half lengthwise to three-fourths from the top, then across.
2. Ask the children to paint these cradles with tempera paints and let dry.
3. Have the children make dolls from clothespins, drawing on faces and pasting on fabric scraps and yarn for clothing.
4. Have the children place the "babies" in the cradles and use extra fabric cut in 10″ squares for blankets. Then let the children play parent/baby for a time with their little creations.

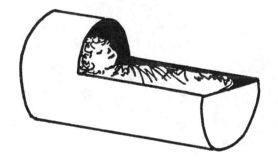

Variations/Ways to Extend:

- Arrange for a parent to bring a baby to the school for a visit. Let the children observe the size of features, capacity for language, motor skills, ways of eating and drinking, and types of food taken. Dust the baby's feet with talcum powder and make a print for the children to compare with their own footprints.
- For background music this week, play "Cradle Song" by Bizet.
- Sing some lullabies with the children. One example is "All the Pretty Little Ponies."

III-38   FAMILY GRAPH

Subject Area: Math

Concepts/Skills: Recognizes the cardinal numerals in sequence
Establishes a one-to-one correspondence

Objectives: The children will interpret a graph showing family size and mark their own places on it.

Materials:
- Large sheet of posterboard
- Felt-tip pen
- Ruler

Procedure:

1. Discuss with the children how many people are in each child's "immediate" family.
2. Draw a large bar graph on the posterboard. Explain that the number of family members is shown by the "up and down" (vertical) column of numbers and the children's names lie on the line going across (horizontal).
3. Help each child fill in his or her bar to show how many people are in his or her family. Show how we can see that there are more people in Tim's family, for example, than in Pam's. Remember, accept the child's view of the number of people in his or her family, making no value judgment.

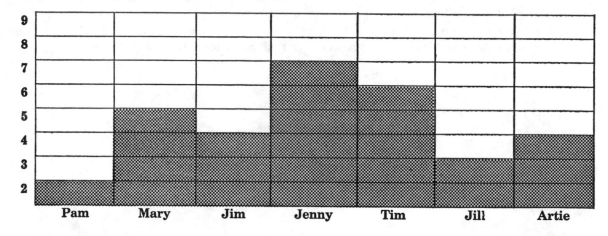

Variation/Way to Extend:

- Encourage dramatic play in the housekeeping corner with extra props related to the family (lots of clothes, accessories, tools, work clothes). Encourage the children to try out different roles: boys helping with shopping, cooking, changing diapers; and girls using tools or fixing a pretend broken faucet.

III-39 LETTERS AND FAMILY PICTURES

Subject Areas: Language Arts and Social Studies

Concepts/Skills: Identifies many letters of the alphabet
Associates a letter with its sound in spoken words

Objective: The children will each construct a sound/picture chart.

Materials:
- Magazines
- Pre-cut letters
- Scissors
- Paste
- Large sheet of posterboard (divided into eight sections) for each child

Procedure:

1. Give each child four letters to paste down the left side of the posterboard.

2. Ask the child to look for family-related pictures in magazines that correspond with each letter sound—for example, M—mother pictures, B—baby pictures, D—daddy pictures, H—home pictures, S—sister pictures, F—family pictures. Have the child paste the picture on the right side of the posterboard next to the proper letter.

Variations/Ways to Extend:

- Conduct a discussion on how each person in a family is special and important. Let each child contribute a special quality about moms, brothers, daddys, and so on.
- Teach the following fingerplay to the children:

  Two little homes, closed up tight, (*close both fists*)
  Open all the windows, let in the light. (*open hands*)
  All the family people, tall and straight, (*straighten all fingers*)
  Ready for school and work, don't be late! (*run fingers up arm*)

- Obtain an 11″ × 14″ art reproduction of "The Sargent Family" (American School, XIX Century, #1265) from the National Gallery of Art, Publications Service, Washington, DC 20565. Be sure to write for a catalog and prices.

III–40 THIS IS THE FAMILY ...

Subject Area: Music

Concepts/Skills: Creates lyrics
Learns and repeats a melody

Objectives: The children will think about family members and create a song reflecting individual responsibilities.

Material: • Tune of "This Is the Way ... "

Procedure:

1. Make up lyrics about the family and the many roles and duties each member has. For example:

   This is the way Daddy rocks the baby, rocks the baby, ...
   This is the way I take out the garbage, take out the garbage, ...
   This is the way Mommy goes to work, goes to work, ...
   This is the way Sister does her homework, does her homework, ...

2. Let the children create their own lyrics for the class to sing.

Variations/Ways to Extend:

• Read *Alexander & the Terrible, Horrible, No Good, Very Bad Day* by Judith Viorst (New York: Atheneum, 1976).
• Listen to "Grandpa Builds a Table" from Hap Palmer's album *Creative Movement and Rhythmic Exploration* (available from Educational Activities, Inc., Box 392, Freeport, NY 11520).

III–41 WHAT'S IN MY HOUSE?

Subject Area: Math

Concepts/Skills: Understands fractions (whole, ½, ¼)
Folds paper into halves and quarters
Uses scissors with control

Objective: The children will assemble a house with sets of furnishings for four rooms.

Materials: • Paper
• Scissors
• Triangles drawn on paper
• Catalogs
• Paste

Procedure:

1. Have the children divide their paper into fourths by folding them in half each way.

2. Let the children cut out the triangles and paste them to the top edge of their folded paper. Explain that they are making their house with a triangular roof and separate rooms.

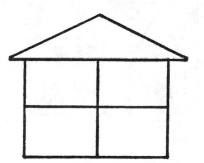

3. Ask the children to decide which rooms they want (kitchen, living room, bedrooms, bathroom, playroom) and then cut furnishings from catalogs and paste them into the appropriate rooms.

Variation/Way to Extend:

• Read *Peter's Chair* by Ezra J. Keats (New York: Harper & Row, 1983).

III–42   BEANBAG HOUSE

Subject Area: Gross Motor Games

Concepts/Skills: Throws a beanbag with direction
Points to and names a circle, square, triangle, and rectangle

Objective: The children will toss a beanbag through cut-out shapes on a cardboard drawing.

Materials: • Two or three neighborhood buildings drawn on cardboard, with geometric cut-outs (circles, squares, triangles, rectangles)
• Beanbags in shapes to match geometric cut-outs

Procedure:

1. Discuss with the children the shapes (names, number of sides, and how to draw). Compare the beanbag shapes with those on each beanbag house.
2. Let the children take turns trying to throw each beanbag through its matching shape on the houses.

Variations/Ways to Extend:

• Encourage the children to predict which shape his or her beanbag will go through before throwing.
• Discuss cleaning the house with the children. Explain that all family members should help to keep a home clean and safe.
• Obtain an 11″ × 14″ art reproduction of "A Girl with a Broom" by Rembrandt van Ryn from the National Gallery of Art, Publications Service, Washington, DC 20565. Be sure to write for a catalog and prices.

III-43 SALTY PHONE NUMBERS

Subject Areas: Social Studies and Language Arts

Concept/Skill: Verbalizes phone number

Objective: The children will use a tactile approach to memorizing their phone numbers.

Materials:
- Salt
- White glue
- Pencil
- Construction paper

Procedure:

1. Write each child's phone number on a piece of construction paper. Go over the numbers with the white glue, repeating the numbers with the child.
2. Allow the children to sprinkle salt on the glue and say each number.
3. When the glue is dry, let the child run his or her fingers over the numbers and practice saying them.

Variations/Ways to Extend:

- Call the local branch of the phone company and inquire about borrowing sets of real telephones for the children to practice dialing and calling home, or dialing their friends' phone numbers.
- Encourage the children to verbalize their full names, addresses, ages, and phone numbers. If allowed by your school, create a class directory of each child's picture, name, address, and telephone number. Review the directory with each child.

III–44 SHAPE NEIGHBORHOOD

Subject Area: Math

Concepts/Skills: Points to and names a circle, square, triangle, and rectangle
Classifies objects by color, shape, and size

Objective: The children will construct collage pictures of their neighborhoods by assembling pre-cut geometric shapes.

Materials:
- Pre-cut geometric paper shapes in red, green, and yellow
- Felt-tip pens
- Paste
- Large sheet of construction paper for each child

Procedure:

1. Discuss with the children how circles, triangles, squares, and rectangles might appear in a neighborhood (the sun, a fir tree, a patio, a building).
2. Give each child about fifteen pre-cut shapes with which to play a sorting game. Have the children separate all the triangles, all the red triangles, all the small red triangles, and so on.
3. Then help the children to paste some of the shapes onto construction paper to make a picture of his or her home and neighborhood. Let the children add details with the pens. Discuss the color and size of the shapes the children are using and put the child's address on his or her picture.

Variations/Ways to Extend:

- Take a walk with the children through the school's neighborhood and look for geometric shapes.
- Read *A Hole Is to Dig* by Ruth Krauss (New York: Harper & Row, 1982).

III–45   NATURE PICTURE PLACEMATS

Subject Area: Art

Concepts/Skills: Expresses self creatively
Predicts realistic outcome of events

Objective: The children will create placemats for their homes from nature materials and crayons.

Materials:
- Old crayons
- Wax paper
- Small plastic pencil sharpener
- Scissors
- Containers
- Newspapers
- Outdoor collage items (small seeds, dry weeds, pine cone pieces, grasses, small leaves, tiny feathers)
- Construction paper
- Iron
- Clear self-stick vinyl

Procedure:

1. Make crayon shavings using old crayons and a plastic pencil sharpener. Do not use too many dark colors. Mix the shavings together and put them in containers.
2. Have each child fold a piece of wax paper in half and sprinkle a few shavings into half of the inside. Have them add some small collage items and then fold the other side of the wax paper on top.
3. Place the pictures between several layers of newspaper and press with a hot iron. (**Caution:** Be sure the children stay away from the heat.) Allow the children to predict what they think will happen to the crayon shavings. (The heat will melt the shavings and seal the two sides of wax paper together.)
4. Add a rectangular construction-paper border to create a placemat and then cover the entire placemat with clear self-stick vinyl. Let each child take home his or her placemat.

Variations/Ways to Extend:

- Use other collage items to express other themes. You might also have the children cut colored tissue paper into desired shapes and place these between the wax paper before sealing.
- Encourage the children to use the block corner to build a neighborhood. Let them embellish the area with cars, figures, and other props that are available.

III–46   AN INDIAN VILLAGE

Subject Area: Social Studies

Concepts/Skills: Expresses self creatively
Manipulates clay into forms and objects

Objective: The children will construct a model Indian village.

Materials:
- Pictures
- Cone-shaped paper cups
- Shirt-sized boxes
- Glue
- Natural objects and feathers
- Felt-tipped pens and crayons
- Plastic straws cut into 3" pieces
- Clay
- Small pieces of cardboard
- Colored fabric
- Scissors

Procedure:

1. Explain to the children that the types of homes built by American Indians varied among Native American nations and depended upon survival needs and regional resources. For example, the Sioux people (Plains) used to live in tepees because they needed to have homes that could be easily moved as they followed herds of buffalo. The Pueblos (Southwest), however, used desert clay mixed with stones and grass to make bricks to build rectangular-shaped houses. The Seminoles (Florida) built their homes on posts, with triangular roofs made of palm leaves and without walls because of the heat. Show the children pictures of these types of homes.

2. Take the children on a walk to a nearby wooded area and collect such natural objects as rocks, tree pieces, bark, shrubbery, and sand. Tell the children that they are going to build Native American villages in shirt-sized boxes.

3. Organize the children into small groups. Have one group construct a Sioux village using paper cups as tepees. Cut pieces of colored fabric into arcs large enough to cover the cone-shaped paper cups. Assist the children in gluing them in place and gluing feathers to the tepee tops as well. Have another group of children build a Pueblo village, using clay to create rectangular-shaped homes. Help a third group of children place four 3" pieces of plastic straw into a clay base and glue a triangular roof (made from a piece of cardboard bent at a 90° angle) onto the straws.

4. Let each village be decorated by the children using felt-tip pens and crayons.

Variation/Way to Extend:

- Read *Little Yellow Fur: Homesteading in 1913* by Wilma P. Hays, new ed. (New York: Coward, 1973).

Special Note:

Use the terms "American Indians" or "Native Americans" when teaching this and the following lessons. Be sensitive to the stereotyping of American Indians by avoiding such phrases as "Sit like an Indian" or "Hop like an Indian."

The activities found in this section attempt to introduce some of the richness of American Indian culture. Realize, however, that there are more than 200 nations, each one separate and distinct.

More information on teaching about Native Americans can be obtained by writing to:

Council on Interracial Books for Children
1841 Broadway
New York, NY 10023
(Ask for *Unlearning "Indian" Stereotypes* and *Books for Equity*)

Mohawk Nation
Rooseveltown, NY 13683
(Ask for posters, booklists, and "Akwesasne Notes")

Instructor Publications
Danville, NY 14437
(Ask for prints, teacher guides, posters, and a catalog)

Native American Educational Program
P.S. 199
West 107 Street
New York, NY 10025
(Ask for information about posters and records)

Museum of the American Indian
Broadway at 155 Street
New York, NY 10032
(Ask for information on slides and books and a catalog)

III–47 BEADED NECKLACE

Subject Area: Art

Concept/Skill: Develops eye–hand coordination

Objective: The children will string beads and paper squares to form a colorful necklace.

Materials:
- Colorful beads
- Lengths of yarn with taped ends
- Small paper squares with hole punched in middle

Procedure:

1. Distribute the beads, paper squares, and yarn to the children. Demonstrate how to push the yarn into the holes and pull through. Say, "Try to make your necklace as beautiful as you can." Encourage multi-colors or colors grouped in sections.
2. Let the children continue until the necklaces are full. Tell the children they can wear them home as American Indian necklaces.

Variations/Ways to Extend:

- Have the children make necklaces by alternating paper squares with dyed macaroni.
- Show pictures (obtained from the previously cited references in Activity III–46) and actual objects (borrowed from a local museum) that Native Americans have created by hand. Such objects can include beadwork, deerskin clothing, rugs, blankets, baskets, jewelry, pottery, and paintings.

III–48   CORN ON THE COB

Subject Areas: Nutrition and Social Studies

Concepts/Skills: Shows an increasing curiosity
Identifies food with its source
Describes salty food by taste

Objectives: The children will shuck, cook, and eat corn.

Materials:
- Fresh corn on the cob
- Salt
- Butter
- Heat source
- Large pot with lid
- Napkins

Procedure:

1. Discuss with the children the important role American Indians played in helping the early Pilgrims survive by showing them how to grow and harvest many foods. Explain that corn was an important staple as a whole food or dried and ground into flour.
2. Have the children help shuck the corn and examine the husks and silk. Then place the cobs into boiling water for about eight minutes. (**Caution:** Be sure the children stay away from the heat.) When the corn is done, let the children enjoy it with butter. Discuss the taste change after adding salt to the corn.

Variations/Ways to Extend:

- Ask a representative of a local county or city museum or historical society to visit the classroom. Have the person discuss and show artifacts about your area's Indian heritage. Make sure the children will be able to handle the items. (You might also contact scout troops for help, too.)
- Try grinding dried corn kernels to make cornmeal. Use this fresh cornmeal in a recipe to make cornbread.
- Read *Little Indian* by Peggy Parish (New York: Simon & Schuster, 1968).

Weekly Subtheme: American Indians

III–49 SYMBOL TEPEES

Subject Area: Art

Concepts/Skills: Understands idea of a tepee as a home
Reproduces a shape
Uses scissors to cut along a line

Objectives: The children will construct tepees and interpret some Indian symbols.

Materials:
- Construction paper
- Paints
- Brushes
- Tape
- Pencils
- Chart
- Twigs and feathers
- Pre-cut cardboard arcs (see pattern)

Procedure:

1. Discuss tepees as one kind of American Indian home that is practical, available, and resourceful.
2. Distribute several pre-cut cardboard arcs for the children to trace onto their construction paper.
3. Display the chart of Indian symbols and ask the children to choose some symbols to copy onto their paper as a design. Then have the children cut out the arc and form a cone. Tape the seam closed.

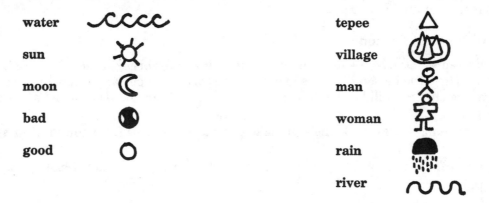

water		tepee	
sun		village	
moon		man	
bad		woman	
good		rain	
		river	

4. Have the children draw a triangle for a door at the bottom of the tepee and cut it out. Tell them that they can put some twigs and feathers through the top opening if they desire.

Variation/Way to Extend:

- Draw the symbols on small pieces of oaktag and encourage the children to create stories by placing the symbols in sequence. You might also have the children use the symbols to create a large mural or to form the pages of a booklet.

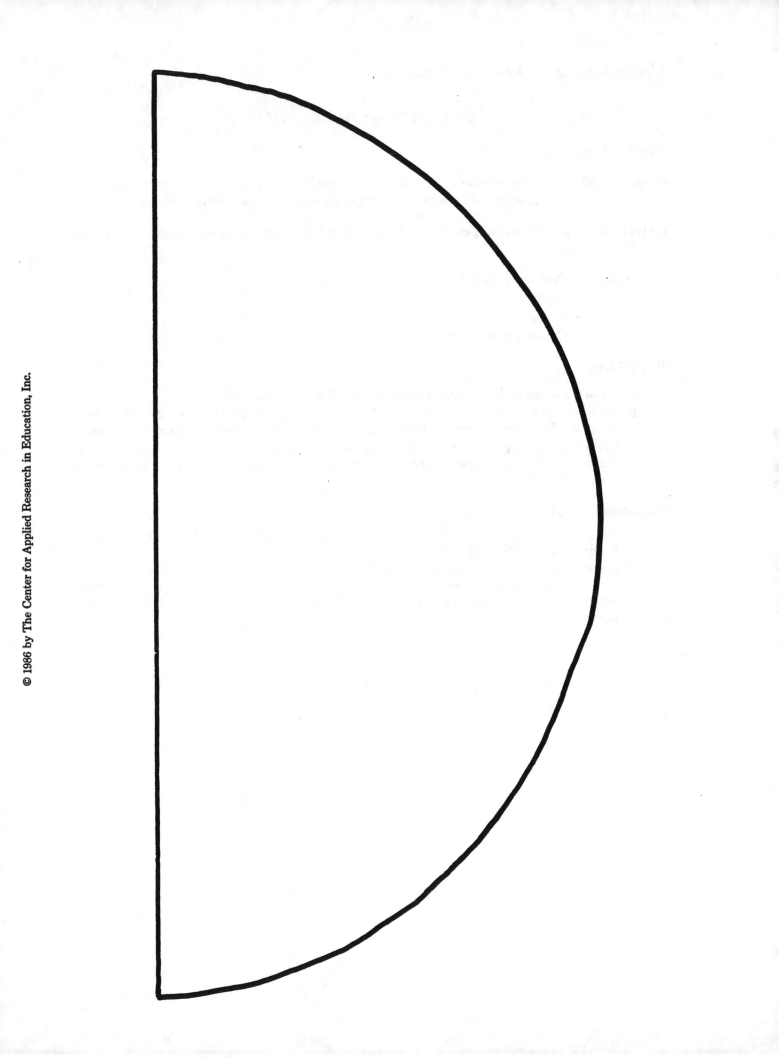

© 1986 by The Center for Applied Research in Education, Inc.

III-50   FUN WITH FEATHERS

Subject Area: Math

Concepts/Skills: Uses scissors with control to cut along a straight line
Identifies a set as a collection of objects having a common property

Objective: The children will cut out feathers that will be used for constructing sets and counting.

Materials:
- Feather shapes (see pattern)
- Scissors
- String
- Construction paper

Procedure:

1. Have the children help you cut out five colored feathers for each child.
2. Give each child a piece of string that when shaped into a circle measures twelve inches in diameter. Demonstrate how to form a circle with the string as the children do likewise.
3. Create a "set" by placing zero or more feathers (up to five) into a circle. Ask the children to create a "set" that is equal to (the same as) your set. Once the set is created, have the children count the feathers.

Variations/Ways to Extend:

- Use numeral cards numbered from one to five. After each child counts the feathers, ask the children to place the appropriate numeral next to the set.
- Have the children make headbands with the feathers. Number them from one to five. Place a 3″ × 24″ strip of red paper on a table in front of each child. Ask the children to place the feathers in sequence and then to paste the ends to the strip of paper. Fit the headband to each child's head and fasten the ends together. Allow the glue to dry.

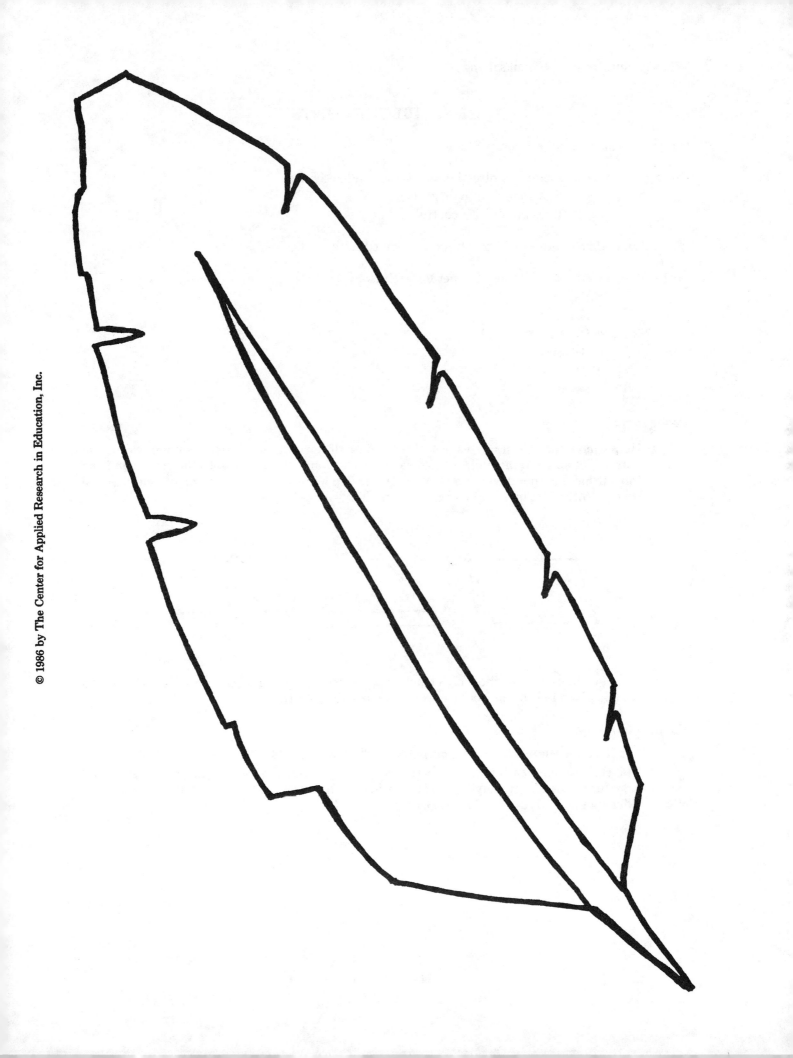

© 1986 by The Center for Applied Research in Education, Inc.

Weekly Subtheme: Thanksgiving

III–51 PILGRIM HATS

Subject Areas: Art and Social Studies

Concepts/Skills: Listens to directions for games and activities
Folds paper into diagonals
Uses brush with control

Objectives: The children will construct and paint Pilgrim hats.

Materials:
- 14″ × 24″ sheet of paper for each child
- Paints
- Brushes
- Gold or silver foil
- Scissors
- Glue
- Stapler

Procedure:

1. Help each child fold a large sheet of paper in half horizontally. Keep the open end at the bottom. Then have the children fold the top right-hand corner down to the center and the top left-hand corner down to meet it. Turn the flap up from the bottom first on one side and then the other. Staple the sides to keep in place.

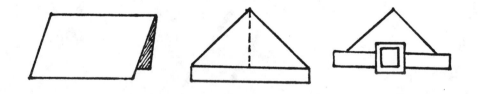

2. Let the children paint their hats black, blue, white, or gray. Tell them that they may add gold or silver foil to the front to resemble a buckle if desired.

Variations/Ways to Extend:

- Let the children use their hats during the "Thanksgiving dinner" in Activity III–52.
- The children can learn more about the story of Thanksgiving by viewing the filmstrip and listening to the accompanying cassette entitled "Thanksgiving Day," available from Kimbo Educational, P.O. Box 477, Long Branch, NJ 07740.

III–52   THANKSGIVING DINNER

Subject Area: Creative Dramatics and Movement

Concepts/Skills: Participates verbally or nonverbally in imaginative play
Makes relevant contributions in small group discussion

Objectives: The children will discuss the first Thanksgiving and participate in a dinner.

Materials:
- Book
- Silverware
- Food (or pictures)
- Napkins

Procedure:

1. Use the Caldecott Honor book *The Thanksgiving Story* by Alice Dalgiesh (New York: Scribner's, 1954) to show the children pictures of the first Thanksgiving. (The text is for older children, but the illustrations effectively portray the occasion.)

2. Following a discussion of the pictures, encourage the children to dramatize a Thanksgiving dinner. Let them set the table by counting silverware and folding napkins. If possible, provide the children with real Thanksgiving foods (sliced turkey, cranberry sauce, and sweet potatoes) and conduct this activity during snack time. (An alternative to real food is using pretend food such as pictures or toy food.) Make real maple syrup popcorn balls for dessert, something the Pilgrim children probably enjoyed, too.

Variations/Ways to Extend:

- Create a "Thankful Book." Have the children cut and paste a picture from a magazine of something for which they are thankful. Encourage each child to dictate a story that you will print under the picture.
- Call local libraries for the purpose of borrowing an art reproduction of John James Audubon's "Wild Turkey" from a collection of prints or in an art or nature book.

III-53   SHORT AND LONG FEATHERS

Subject Area: Math

Concepts/Skills: Places items in order and compares size differences
Points to and names colors
Uses scissors with control

Objectives: The children will place paper strips in order by size and then use them to decorate turkeys.

Materials:
• Construction paper in six basic colors
• Scissors
• Pre-cut turkey shape for each child
• Glue
• Paper cutter

Procedure:

1. Use a paper cutter to cut red, orange, yellow, green, blue, and violet paper into strips to be used as turkey feathers. (**Caution:** Be sure the children stay away from the cutting edge.) Vary the length of each color so that the red strips are shorter than the orange ones, which are shorter than the yellow ones, and so on through the six colors.
2. Give each child one strip of each color and have the children place them in order by size. Tell them to begin with the red and then find the next longer paper, then the next, until the strips are in sequence from shortest to longest.
3. Help the children to cut slits along the strips' sides to resemble feathers and then glue the feathers (however they want) onto their turkey's back.

Variations/Ways to Extend:

• Provide the children with good, clear photographs of turkeys to look at this week.
• Read *The Bears Find Thanksgiving* by John Barrett (Chicago: Childrens Press, 1981).

III-54 WALDORF SALAD

Subject Area: Nutrition

Concept/Skill: Describes foods by taste

Objective: The children will learn to enjoy some foods that the Pilgrims and Indians had together.

Materials:
- 4 apples, diced
- 1 cup walnut meats, chopped
- 4 stalks celery, cut in small pieces
- 1 cup lowfat yogurt
- Lettuce leaves
- Bowls
- Forks

Procedure:

1. Discuss Thanksgiving and ask the children what they are thankful for. Also talk about traditional holiday foods, such as turkeys, pumpkins, apples, nuts, celery, onions, potatoes, and cranberries. Explain to the children that *three* of these foods will be used to make a salad.
2. With the children's help, mix the apples, celery, and nuts together with the yogurt and serve over lettuce leaves at snack time. Encourage the children to describe the flavors.

Variation/Way to Extend:

- Listen to "Things I'm Thankful For" from Hap Palmer's album *Holiday Songs and Rhythms* (available from Educational Activities, Inc., Box 392, Freeport, NY 11520).

III-55 TURKEY FINGERPLAY

Subject Area: Language Arts

Concepts/Skills: Verbalizes a fingerplay
Orally labels pictures

Objective: The children will demonstrate the actions to a fingerplay about a turkey.

Materials:
- Words to the fingerplay
- Pictures

Procedure:

1. Display several large colorful pictures of turkeys for the children to look at.
2. Teach the following fingerplay to the children:

> There was a turkey, very fat (*spread out hands to make fat turkey*)
> Who loved to gobble, gobble.
> But when he'd make that funny sound,
> His head would wobble, wobble! (*bob head up and down*)
>
> He loves to spread his tail out wide, (*spread fingers on hands*)
> His wattle is so bright, (*stroke neck*)
> Between the wobble and the wattle,
> He's such a funny sight!

Variations/Ways to Extend:

- If possible, visit a turkey farm for first-hand observations of wobbles and wattles.
- Give each child a small turkey shape outlined in heavy marker on brown construction paper. Let the children cut these out and paste them onto cardboard squares. Next provide them with a mixture of spices to glue onto their turkeys as feathers. Use cinnamon bark, cloves, allspice, and citrus peel. Point out the strong, sweet scent to the children.

THE SPIRIT OF THE SEASON

○ Giving and Sharing

○ Holiday Games

○ Children Around the World

○ Holiday Foods and Traditions

III–56   SANTA MOBILE

Subject Area: Art

Concepts/Skills: Explores new materials
Develops fine motor movements of cutting, pasting, and taping

Objective: The children will construct a three-part Santa to hang as a mobile.

Materials:
- Small styrofoam balls
- Paper plates
- Black shiny paper
- Red tempera paint
- Brushes
- Tape
- Dental floss or fishline
- Cotton
- Scissors
- Silver paper
- Red construction paper
- Markers
- Large needle

Procedure:

1. Cut out red hats and black boots. Let the children cut silver and black strips for belts and buckles and set aside.
2. Have the children paste the red hats onto the styrofoam balls and use cotton for beards. Let them use markers to draw facial features.
3. Help the children paint the front and back of the paper plates red. Allow the paint to dry. Then have the children glue on the black belts and silver buckles.
4. Thread a large needle with dental floss or fishline and push it through the top of the styrofoam head and out the neck area. Tape this part to one edge of a paper plate. Then tape other short pieces of fishline to the paper plate and to each of the two black boots.
5. Let the children fill in details as desired. Then hang the mobiles as decorations or send them home as gifts for parents, siblings, and friends.

Variations/Ways to Extend:

- If styrofoam balls are unavailable, use small white paper plates as heads. Write a holiday message in black marker on the back of a red paper plate or reproduce a holiday poem and let each child paste it onto the back of the plate.
- Provide markers, crayons, and paper and let the children draw and color their own versions of Santa Claus.

Weekly Subtheme: Giving and Sharing

III-57 HOLIDAY CARDS

Subject Area: Social Studies

Concepts/Skills: Folds and creases paper two times
Verbalizes a ditty
Uses scissors with control to cut on a line

Objectives: The children will construct a holiday card and follow the procedure for sending it through the mail.

Materials:
- White paper
- Words to ditty
- Glue
- Markers
- Shapes drawn on paper
- Scissors
- Glitter
- Pre-addressed envelopes
- Postage stamps

Procedure:

1. Give the children sheets of white paper and demonstrate how to fold them in half and in half again to make holiday cards.

2. Let the children select one holiday shape that has been drawn on paper. Have each child cut out his or her own shape and paste it onto the front of the card.

3. Help the children squeeze glue where glitter is desired and then sprinkle the glitter onto those places. Collect the excess glitter on a large sheet of paper so that it may be saved and reused.

4. Say the following ditty to the children and encourage them to repeat it:

   Happy Holidays to you,
   I love you, I do!

5. Give each child a copy of the ditty written on a small piece of paper that can be glued inside the card. Then help each child write his or her name inside the card.

6. Help the children insert the holiday cards in pre-addressed envelopes and stamp them. If possible, walk to a mailbox and mail the cards home to the children's families.

7. Discuss with the children how letters and cards can be sent through the mail to loved ones and how letter carriers deliver the mail.

Variation/Way to Extend:

- Have the children use crayons to decorate the holiday card around the picture and ditty. You might ask the children to dictate "Why I love you" stories about their parents; these can be written on the inside cover.

III-58 PINE CONE PRESENTS

Subject Area: Science

Concepts/Skills: Demonstrates senses of touch, smell, and sight
Speaks in sentences of six words
Listens to directions for activities

Objectives: The children will closely examine pine cones and construct pine cone presents.

Materials:
- Pine cones
- Magnifying glasses
- Glue
- Paper
- Glitter
- String or pipe cleaners
- Paper plates
- Marker
- Box

Procedure:

1. Take the children to an outdoor area where they can each collect at least two pine cones. Encourage the children to look at, feel, and smell the pine cones.

2. Back in the classroom, have the children use magnifying glasses to compare their two pine cones. Ask them to note likenesses and differences.

3. Explain to the children that seeds are in the pine cones and that these seeds grow into new little trees if planted. Tell the children that they are going to use the pine cones to make pretty holiday decorations and presents that can be given to others to make them happy.

4. Let each child decorate his or her pine cones by placing puddles of glue on paper plates, rolling their cones in the glue, and then sprinkling glitter onto the pine cones until they are shiny. (Be sure to provide many different colors of glitter.) Tie string or pipe cleaners around the top of each cone so that it can be hung.

5. Write the name of each child on a piece of paper and place the names in a box. Ask each child to come up to the box to select a name and give the selected child the pine cone present he or she has made. Encourage such vocabulary as "I made this. I hope you like it," "Thank you," and so on.

Variations/Ways to Extend:
- Help the children make a collage of pine branches and extra cones.
- Let the children decorate a class Christmas tree with their glittery pine cones.

III–59   SANTA BULLETIN BOARD

Subject Area: Language Arts

Concepts/Skills: Makes relevant verbal contribution in small group discussion
Uses scissors with control

Objectives: The children will mount pictures of holiday gifts and select their favorite present.

Materials: • Red and green construction paper
• Magazines
• Glue
• Scissors
• Bulletin board display

Procedure:

1. Create a bulletin board of a large Santa Claus with a cotton beard and sack. Behind Santa, place a sheet of white butcher paper about twelve inches wide and cut scroll-like with "Dear Santa" written on it.

2. Provide the children with magazines and scissors. Tell them to look for pictures of what they would like to give and receive as holiday gifts and to cut them out. Assist each child in gluing the pictures on a piece of green or red construction paper and ask the child to complete the sentences "My favorite present would be _____ " and "I would like to give my _____ a _____ ." Write these sentences, along with the child's name, at the bottom of the paper.

3. Display each child's completed gift list on the bulletin board.

Variation/Way to Extend:

• Sing "Santa Claus Is Coming to Town" with the children.

Weekly Subtheme: Giving and Sharing

III-60 PRETENDING

Subject Area: Creative Dramatics

Concept/Skill: Participates in verbal and nonverbal imaginative play

Objective: The children will act out various giving and sharing behaviors through pantomime.

Materials: • Props

Procedure:

1. Tell the children that they are going to play a game called "Pretending." Have each child demonstrate, through pantomime, a giving or sharing behavior while the others try to guess what the child is doing. Provide props when needed.

2. Whisper the following suggestions to the children involved in the pretending:

   Make a cake and give it to a friend.
   With a friend, look for a Christmas tree and chop it down.
   Light the menorah.
   Wrap a present for a friend.
   Decorate a tree with a friend.
   Play games with a dreidel.
   Eat a holiday dinner with family.

3. As the children act out the situation, help the others to guess accurately by giving clues and hints. Ask the children to suggest other ideas to convey through pantomime.

Variation/Way to Extend:

   • Have the children make holiday necklace presents for one another by cutting pictures from old holiday cards, punching a hole in each one, and inserting string through the hole.

III-61 RUDOLPH IN THE MIDDLE

Subject Area: Music

Concepts/Skills: Verbalizes a song
Listens to directions for a game
Works and plays cooperatively with other children
Stops moving upon command

Objective: The children will participate in a tag game.

Materials: • None

Procedure:

1. Ask all the children, except for one, to form a circle. Tell the one child not in the circle that he or she is Rudolph the Red-Nosed Reindeer and should stand in the center of the circle.
2. Have the other children walk hand in hand around the child and sing the first four lines of "Rudolph the Red-Nosed Reindeer."
3. Tell the children that as soon as they finish singing the word *glows*, they must all sit down. The child in the middle is to attempt to tag any other child before he or she sits. Whoever is tagged then stands in the center as Rudolph and continues the game.

Variation/Way to Extend:

• Sing "Merry Christmas to You" and "Happy Hanukkah to You" to the tune of "Happy Birthday to You." Let the children accompany their singing with rhythm instruments.

III-62   TASTY TREATS

Subject Area: Thinking Games

Concept/Skill: Describes objects by taste (sweet, sour, salty)

Objective: The children will identify the appropriate taste.

Materials: • Sweet, sour, and salty foods

Procedure:

1. Bring in three foods that represent sweet, sour, and salty tastes and are associated with the holiday season. For example, you might want to use dates (sweet), lemon sour balls (sour), and popcorn (salty).
2. Have the children play a game called "Tasty Treats." Let each child take a turn putting on a blindfold. Give the blindfolded child one of the three kinds of food and ask him or her to taste it and say if it is sweet, sour, or salty.

Variations/Ways to Extend:

- After each child has had a turn with "Tasty Treats," play a tag game. One child, "It," must attempt to tag one of the other children who are safe as long as they are holding hands. Encourage the children holding hands to run to other children as a way of allowing "It" an opportunity to tag someone.
- Thread leftover popcorn on fishline and use this as a holiday decoration.

III-63   MUSICAL CHAIRS

Subject Area: Gross Motor Games

Concept/Skill: Stops moving upon command

Objective: The children will play "Musical Chairs" to a holiday song.

Materials:
- Record
- Phonograph
- Chairs

Procedure:

1. Play holiday music, such as "Jingle Bells," while the children walk around the outside of chairs arranged in a circle, one foot apart from one another. Be sure to place the *same* number of chairs as there are children.

2. As the children are walking, stop the music at different times. Each time the music stops, have the children scramble to find an empty seat. Do *not* eliminate chairs or children because four-year-olds should not be made to engage in a competitive game with winners and losers.

Variations/Ways to Extend:

- Play a recording of "March of the Toys" by Victor Herbert and let the children move around like wooden soldiers.
- Play a recording of "Toy Symphony" by Haydn and allow the children to move around like toy robots.

III-64 PLAYFUL DECORATIONS

Subject Area: Math

Concepts/Skills: Uses scissors with control to cut on a line
Counts from one to ten
Moves body creatively

Objectives: The children will construct decorated Christmas trees and play games with them.

Materials:
- Green construction paper
- Collage materials
- Glue
- Pencils
- Pre-cut strips of gold foil

Procedure:

1. Draw triangular trees on construction paper and assist the children in cutting them out. Glue on the gold foil as garlands.
2. Provide the children with collage materials—such as cotton balls, strips of red paper, felt scraps, yarn, buttons, and foil pieces—to glue onto their tree shapes.
3. Once the collages are completed, ask the children to sit in a circle. With the Christmas trees in hand, spread out three of them on the floor in the middle of the circle. Call on children one at a time to count the number of trees. Then assign a physical movement to each number, such as hop three times, take two giant steps (forward or backward), hop on one or two feet, or leap frog (with another child), and ask the children to perform it.
4. Continue the game by providing different numbers of trees. When finished, use the trees as room decorations.

Variation/Way to Extend:

- Give each child a green triangle cut from construction paper and ask the children to think of all the things they can do with this triangle, such as hop on it, jump over it, walk around it, and so on. Accept all feasible answers and give praise for such ingenious answers as "Use it for a kite" or "Make a beard from it."

III-65 FROSTY PUPPETS

Subject Area: Language Arts

Concepts/Skills: Laces a series of holes
  Plays cooperatively with other children
  Creatively expresses self orally

Objectives: The children will make hand puppets and use them to engage in conversational play.

Materials:
- White felt squares
- White yarn
- Blunt plastic tapestry needles with large eyes
- Hole puncher
- Table
- Props (optional)
- Scrap material
- Assorted buttons
- Glue
- Black felt-tip pens
- Puppet shape (see pattern)
- Scissors

Procedure:

1. Use the pattern to cut out two sheets of white felt for each child. Punch holes all around the figure as shown.
2. Help the children thread the large-eye tapestry needles with white yarn and sew their felt pieces together. Then have them glue shiny button eyes and felt noses in place. Let them use black felt-tip pens to add mouths. Encourage the children to add colored buttons, black felt hats, and tiny scrap material scarves as accessories.
3. Have the children put their hands inside the puppets to make the snowmen nod their heads, clap or wave their hands, bow, climb, talk, laugh, and cry.
4. Turn a table onto its side to use as a stage that the children can get behind. Let a few children at a time make their puppets play and talk together. Use props if desired.

Variations/Ways to Extend:

- Make more puppets for other characters seen at this time of year. Provide lots of scrap materials and let the children create puppets of their own design.
- Use instrumental holiday music to set the mood for the puppet plays that may result.

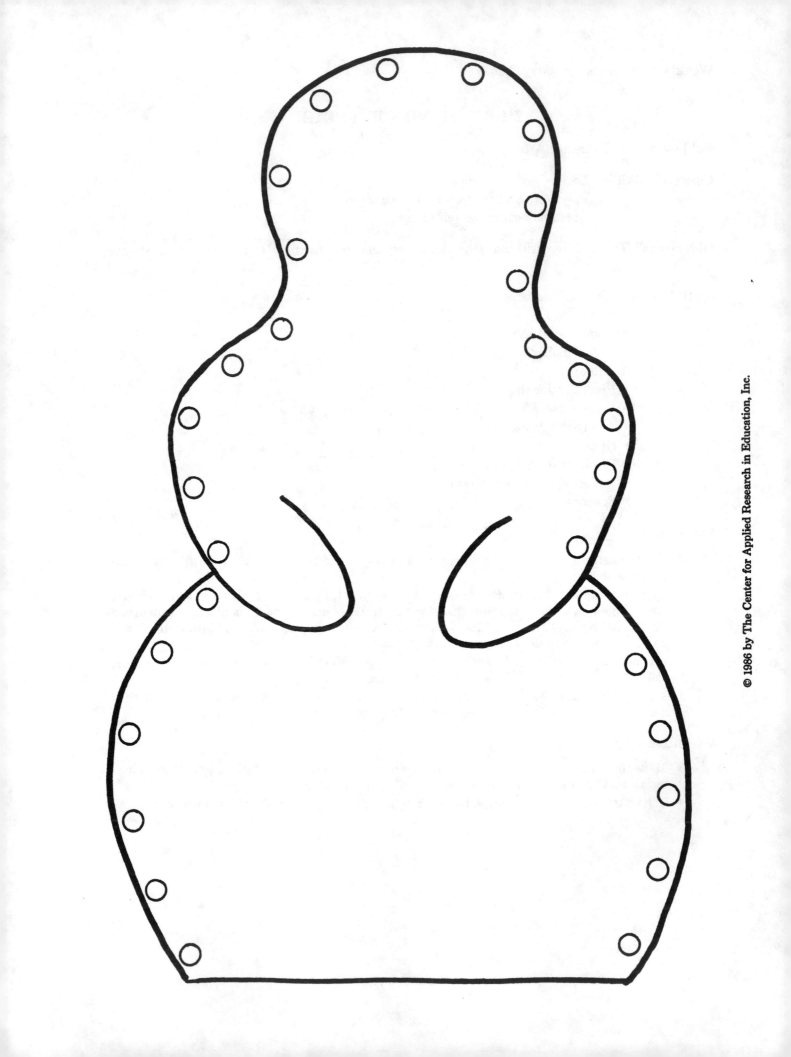

© 1986 by The Center for Applied Research in Education, Inc.

III-66   CHRISTMAS IN FRANCE

Subject Area: Art

Concepts/Skills: Interprets the main idea of a story
Uses scissors with control to cut on a curved line
Places pictures in time-sequence order to tell a story

Objectives: The children will cut out and color pictures of wooden shoes.

Materials: • Book
• White construction paper
• Newsprint
• Scissors
• Pre-cut shoe shape (see pattern)
• Globe
• Crayons

Procedure:

1. Read *Noel for Jeanne-Marie* by Françoise (New York: Scribner's, 1953). This is the story of a little girl in the south of France and how she enjoys Christmas. Show the children on the globe where they and you live and where France is located. Explain to the children that the children in France leave their shoes out on Christmas Eve and wake up to find them filled with presents.

2. After reading and discussing the story, let the children trace the shoe pattern onto white construction paper. Help them each to cut out two shoes and choose their own crayons for coloring.

3. Once this is completed, help the children glue the shoes onto a large sheet of newsprint. On another sheet of paper, let each child draw a picture of a desired gift, cut it out, and glue it to the shoe opening for a decorative display.

4. Now make copies of three different pages from *Noel for Jeanne-Marie*. Ask the children to put these in order (from left to right) according to when they happened in the story. Encourage further practice of putting other pages from the book in sequence.

Variations/Ways to Extend:

• Have the children count all the shoes. Display the newsprint and decorate with mistletoe. Explain to the children that in France, mistletoe is hung above the doorway to bring luck during the year.

• Read the poem "Near and Far" by Kate Cox Goodard, found in *Poems to Read to the Very Young*, selected by Josette Frank and illustrated by E. Wilkin (New York: Random House, 1982). It is about children in various lands appearing different but being similar inside.

• Explain that in Holland, children place their wooden shoes in front of the fireplace on St. Nicholas' Eve (December 5). They put hay and carrots in the shoes for St. Nicholas's horse. If the children have been good, they receive candy in their shoes; if not, St. Nicholas will leave them coal. When the shoe display comes down, let the children staple their wooden shoe cut-outs together. Place candy pieces in them for the children to take home.

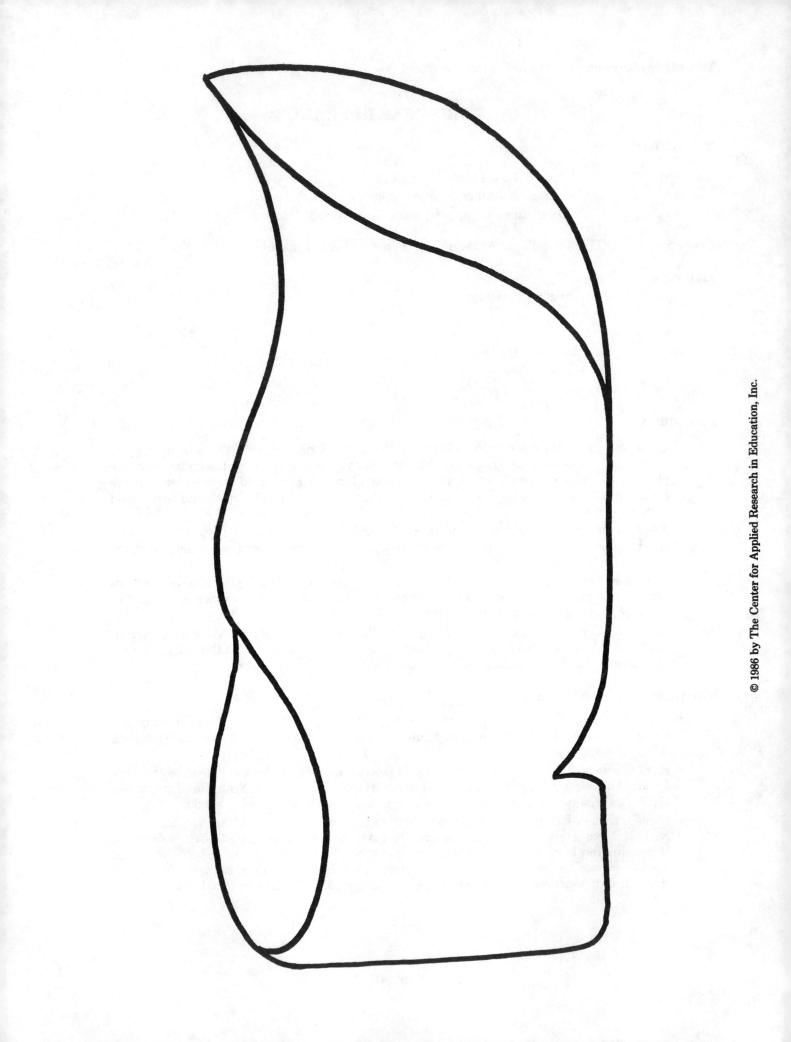

© 1986 by The Center for Applied Research in Education, Inc.

III-67 HANUKKAH *LATKES*

Subject Area: Nutrition and Foods Experience

Concepts/Skills: Labels common items
Understands full, half full, and empty
Understands fractions (½, ¼, whole)

Objectives: The children will identify ingredients, measure them, and create a favorite Hanukkah recipe.

Materials:
- 2 cups peeled potatoes, grated
- 1 tablespoon flour
- 1 teaspoon wheat germ
- ½ tablespoon baking powder
- 1 beaten egg
- ⅛ teaspoon minced parsley
- ⅛ teaspoon chopped onion
- Salt
- Pepper

- Apple sauce, sour cream, and cinnamon
- Margarine
- Bowl
- Electric fry pan
- Ladle
- Plates
- Paper towels
- Forks
- Spoons

Procedure:

1. Explain to the children that Hanukkah is a Jewish holiday celebrated at approximately the same time that Christians observe Christmas. Also explain that *latkes* (potato pancakes) are often served during Hanukkah.

2. Gather the material needed, identify each ingredient, and let the children help you make the *latkes*. Place the potatoes in a bowl. (In order to avoid discoloration, keep the grated potatoes in a bowl of cold water until two cups have been attained.) Add the flour, baking powder, wheat germ, egg, minced parsley, chopped onion, and a dash of salt and pepper. Mix the ingredients thoroughly. Then form thin pancakes on a greased electric fry pan. (**Caution:** Be sure the children stay away from the heat.) Cook at 350° F for two to three minutes on each side, until brown. Drain the pancakes on paper towels before serving.

3. Let the children enjoy the *latkes* with apple sauce, cinnamon, or sour cream. Provide all three so that the children may experience each one.

Variations/Ways to Extend:

- Show pictures of the ways Hanukkah and Christmas are celebrated (Christmas trees, menorahs, presents, *dreidels*). Let the children describe their experiences if they want.
- Choose a recipe from *Many Hands Cooking: An International Cookbook for Girls and Boys* by Terry T. Cooper and Marilyn Ratner (New York: Thomas Y. Crowell and the U.S. Committee for UNICEF, 1974). Let the children help you in the preparation of the food.
- While the children are enjoying the *latkes*, play the song "The Hanukkah Song" from the album *Holiday Songs for All Occasions* by Jill Galina (available from Kimbo Educational, P.O. Box 477, 86 South 5th Avenue, Long Branch, NJ 07740).

III-68 SPEAKING SPANISH

Subject Area: Language Arts

Concepts/Skills: Predicts realistic outcome of events
Makes relevant verbal contribution in a small group discussion

Objectives: The children will suggest what the story character should do and also learn some Spanish words.

Materials:
- Globe
- Pictures

Procedure:

1. Show the children on a globe where Mexico is located and display some pictures of Mexican people, streets, markets, and so on.
2. Tell the following story to the children: "Little Timmy is on a trip to Mexico with his parents. They go shopping in a large, open market that is very crowded. Timmy smells the enchiladas and burritos cooking and wanders in the direction of the delicious smells. Soon, he is lost. Timmy speaks only English, and all the people around him are speaking Spanish. What should Timmy do?"
3. After the children make some suggestions, ask them if they would like to learn some Spanish words. Teach the following:

   Buenos dias (Hello)
   Buenas noches (Good night)
   Hasta luego (See you soon)
   Feliz Navidad (Merry Christmas)
   Ajudame (Help me)

Variation/Way to Extend:

- Read the Caldecott Honor book *Pedro, the Angel of Olvera Street* by Leo Politi (New York: Scribner's, 1946).

III-69   JAPANESE PARTY

Subject Area: Creative Dramatics and Movement

Concept/Skill: Participates verbally in imaginative play

Objective: The children will dramatize a Japanese party by eating and dressing as Japanese people do.

Materials: • Kimonos
   • Blender
   • Bananas
   • Milk
   • Oranges
   • Rice cakes
   • Cups
   • Napkins
   • Haiku samples

Procedure:

1. Set up the dramatic play area as a Japanese dining area. If possible, dress the children in the traditional costume of Japan called the kimono. Have the children take off their shoes.

2. Together with the children, make a drink of peeled oranges, bananas, and milk that is mixed in a blender. Let the children enjoy this drink with rice (*mochi*) cakes.

3. While the children are eating, softly recite your own Haiku (unrhymed Japanese poems of three lines—five syllables, seven syllables, and five syllables, respectively) holiday poems. Explain that the Japanese speak softly during meals. Encourage the children to use the words *kimono* and *mochi*.

Variations/Ways to Extend:

• Obtain free pictures of Japanese family life and fact sheets by contacting:

   Japan Information Center
   Consulate General of Japan
   299 Park Avenue, 18th Floor
   New York, NY 10171
   (212) 371-8222

   Share these pictures with the children.

• Read the Caldecott Honor book *Crow Boy* by Taro Yashima (New York: Viking, 1955).

III–70 PAPIER-MÂCHÉ PIÑATA

Subject Areas: Art and Social Studies

Concept/Skill: Works cooperatively with others

Objective: The children will learn about a Mexican holiday tradition by creating a piñata.

Materials:
- Paper towels
- String
- Paper
- Paints
- Brushes
- Balloon
- Flour
- Water
- Globe
- Snack foods
- Plastic bag
- Tape
- Egg carton sections
- Cardboard dowels

Procedure:

1. Explain to the children that a piñata is a decorated pottery jar, frequently in the shape of a donkey, filled with candies, fruits, and gifts, that is hung from the ceiling. It is broken as part of Mexican Christmas activities. Show the children on a globe where you and they live and then show where Mexico is located.

2. Let the children help you prepare the paste by using the proportion of ⅓ cup flour to ¼ cup water. (To avoid a mess, place the mixture in a plastic bag and knead.)

3. Inflate a balloon. Dip pieces of paper towels into the paste and place them on the balloon, covering it entirely. Let dry.

4. Roll a ball of paper as the donkey's head, tape it to the balloon, and cover it with toweling dipped in the paste. For ears, tape and cover egg carton sections. Tape on cardboard dowels for legs and also cover with wet toweling.

5. Allow two days for the paste to dry and then paint it. Add the facial features of a donkey.

6. Carefully break into the top of the covered balloon and fill the cavity with nuts, popcorn, sugarless gum, and other candies and small gifts. Hang the piñata from the ceiling if possible.

7. On the last day of school before the holiday recess, allow the children to sing the song below, break open the piñata, and share the treats.

> "Break the Piñata"
> (to the tune of "Mary Had a Little Lamb")
> Let's all break the piñ-a-ta, piñ-a-ta, piñ-a-ta,
> Let's all break the piñ-a-ta
> And share its candy and gifts.

Variations/Ways to Extend:

- If the papier-mâché project is too lengthy, use smaller paper bags filled with treats and decorated as animals. Let the children decorate the bags as make-believe animals using cut fringed paper strips or feathers and by coloring on facial features.

- While the children enjoy their treats from the piñata, let them listen to a recording of Ravel's "Bolero."

III–71   LITTLEST ANGEL, BIGGEST STAR

Subject Area: Art

Concepts/Skills: Listens to a story of at least ten minutes in length
Develops fine motor movement of cutting on a line

Objectives: The children will listen to a story and construct a star.

Materials: • Book
• Scissors
• Star shape (see pattern)
• Hole puncher
• Cardboard
• Pencils
• Yarn
• Heavy-duty aluminum foil
• Glue
• Glitter

Procedure:

1. Read *The Littlest Angel* by Charles Tazewell (Chicago: Childrens Press, 1946). This is a beautiful book for four-year-olds about the star of Bethlehem arising from the angel's little treasure box; however, it is long, so you might want to read it in two sittings.
2. Cut a star from cardboard for each child. Give each child two squares of aluminum foil that are big enough to cover the star. Glue a piece of foil to each side of the star shape and let the children cut around it to form a shiny star.
3. Help the children spread some glue on each side of the foil-covered star and sprinkle with multi-colored glitter. Allow to dry. Then punch a hole in the star's top point and string with red yarn to hang as an ornament.

Variation/Way to Extend:

• Use refrigerator-dough cookies as a base and star-shaped cookie cutters to make star cookies for today's snack. Let the children use colored sprinkles to decorate the cookies before baking.

© 1986 by The Center for Applied Research in Education, Inc.

III-72 HOLIDAY FRUIT SALAD

Subject Area: Nutrition and Foods Experience

Concepts/Skills: Develops fine motor movement of cutting fruit with a plastic knife

Labels common items (fruits)

Objectives: The children will assist in making a fruit salad and share it with others.

Materials:
- Apples
- Bananas
- Tangerines
- Canned pineapple
- Seedless grapes
- Pears
- Canned peaches
- Cutting board
- Sturdy plastic knives
- Large bowl
- Paper cups
- Plastic spoons

Procedure:

1. Send home a note requesting that the children contribute by a designated date a particular fruit for the Holiday Fruit Salad.
2. After washing the fruit, ask the children to identify the fruits. Explain how they will each contribute (give) their fruit so that a *big* fruit salad can be made for everyone.
3. Help the children cut the fruit on the cutting board with the plastic knives and place the slices in a large bowl. Invite another class in for a snack and explain how the children are sharing their fruits. Let the children help serve the fruit salad in cups.

Variations/Ways to Extend:

- Play "Food Riddles." Describe one of the fruits made in the fruit salad and have the children guess the correct fruit. For example, "I'm thinking of a fruit that is red and round and has seeds in the middle."
- Obtain an 11″ × 14″ art reproduction of "Still Life with Apples and Peaches" by Paul Cézanne from the National Gallery of Art, Publications Service, Washington, DC 20565. Be sure to write for a catalog and prices.

III-73   HOW WOULD YOU TREAT SANTA?

Subject Areas: Language Arts and Creative Dramatics/Movement

Concepts/Skills: Predicts realistic outcomes of events
Listens to a story
Participates verbally in imaginative play

Objectives: The children will listen to a story and dramatize scenes from it.

Materials: • Book
• Props

Procedure:

1. Discuss with the children the tradition of Christmas Eve—that is, leaving cookies and milk for Santa Claus, who will bring presents to each child's house while he or she is asleep.
2. Read *Wake Up, Bear . . . It's Christmas!* by Stephen Gammell (New York: Lothrop, 1981) or a similar book. *Wake Up, Bear* is about an animal that meets Santa Claus on Christmas Eve and doesn't know who he is but proceeds to invite him in to warm up. Santa then takes the bear for a ride.
3. After reading and discussing the story with the children, ask, "What would you do if you met Santa Claus on Christmas Eve and he was cold, hungry, and very tired?" Make props available, such as Santa's hat, a cot, and snacks, and guide the children through a dramatic play recreation of the story read to them.

Variation/Way to Extend:

• Let the children do a watercolor picture of a scene they remember from the book.

III-74 HOLIDAY SNACK

Subject Area: Math

Concepts/Skills: Understands fractions (½, ¼)
Counts from one to ten

Objective: The children will apply math skills in preparing a nutritious snack.

Materials:
- Ingredients
- Saucepan
- Spoons
- Measuring cup
- Wax paper
- Heat source

Procedure:

1. Allow the children to assist you in identifying and measuring out the following ingredients and placing them in a saucepan:

   1 cup sugar
   ¼ cup butter or margarine
   ½ cup evaporated milk
   ¼ cup crunchy peanut butter
   ½ teaspoon vanilla
   1 cup oats
   ½ cup Spanish peanuts

2. Heat the first three ingredients in a saucepan to boiling, stirring constantly. **(Caution: Be sure the children stay away from the heat.)** Remove the saucepan from the heat and mix in the peanut butter and vanilla. Then stir in the oats and nuts.

3. Drop small tablespoons of the mixture onto wax paper and shape like chocolate kisses. (If the mixture becomes too stiff, stir in one or two drops of milk.) Let stand until firm.

4. Point out to the children the transformation of the candy mixture from a liquid to a solid and have them count the kisses in groups of ten. Then serve the candies and enjoy.

Variation/Way to Extend:

- Pop popcorn and have each child measure ½ cup and place it in a plastic bag. Then ask the children to each count five raisins and five peanuts and place them into other plastic bags. Put all of the plastic bags into a larger brown bag. At snack time, let the children reach into the brown bag with their eyes closed and pick up a surprise treat bag of either popcorn or peanuts/raisins.

III-75 CHRISTMAS COOKIES

Subject Area: Nutrition and Foods Experience

Concepts/Skills: Develops fine motor movements of measuring, pouring, and rolling
Enjoys a process and a finished product

Objectives: The children will help prepare and bake holiday cookies.

Materials: (This recipe makes three dozen cookies)
- 2 cups flour
- 1¼ cups softened butter
- ½ cup sugar
- 2 egg yolks
- ½ cup finely chopped walnuts
- Strawberry jam
- Bowl
- Spoons
- Cookie sheets
- Oven

Procedure:

1. Combine the first five ingredients and mix to a smooth dough. Let the dough stand for thirty minutes.
2. Ask the children to pinch off small handfuls of dough and shape them into little balls. Have each child press a finger into the centers and fill the indentations with jam.
3. Bake the cookies on greased cookie sheets at 350° F for fifteen minutes or until lightly browned. (**Caution:** Be sure the children stay away from the heat.)
4. Let the children enjoy the cookies with milk or juice at snack time.

Variation/Way to Extend:

- Teach the children the traditional German holiday song "O Christmas Tree." Complete words and music can be found in *The Great Song Book* by Timothy John, edited by John Hankey (New York: Doubleday, 1978).

  O Christmas tree, O Christmas tree,
  Your branches green delight us.
  O Christmas tree, O Christmas tree,
  Your branches green delight us.
  They're green when summer days are bright,
  They're green when winter snow is white.
  O Christmas tree, O Christmas tree,
  Your branches green delight us.

WINTER

- ○ Getting a Fresh Start
- ○ Health and Safety
- ○ Snow
- ○ Water and Ice

Weekly Subtheme: Getting a Fresh Start

III–76 WHAT IF?

Subject Area: Thinking Game

Concepts/Skills: Predicts realistic outcomes of events

Understands that people wear appropriate clothing for protection from extremes of weather.

Objective: The children will predict answers to questions about the new year and wintertime.

Material: • List of situations thought up in advance

Procedure:

1. Generate a host of "What if" questions pertaining to the January theme. Some examples are:

    What if it is very cold outside and you forget your mittens?

    What if no one shoveled the snow off the walkway to your front door and then you tried to go out?

    What if you build a snowman and the next day the sun comes out very warm and bright?

    What if it never rained?

    What if we didn't change and grow?

Variation/Way to Extend:

• Read *Everything Changes* by Ruth R. Howell (New York: Atheneum, 1968).

III-77 SEASON BOOK

Subject Area: Math

Concepts/Skills: Observes seasonal changes

Distinguishes between concepts of "some," "most," and "all"

Objective: The children will demonstrate knowledge of the four seasons by constructing a book of original drawings.

Materials: • Pictures of the seasons
• Paper
• Crayons

Procedure:

1. Discuss the four seasons of the year. Recall the recent fall holidays to help the children understand sequence and time's passing. Show pictures of the seasons and talk about familiar experiences that occur during each.

2. Let the children draw a picture of what they do during each season. Then make the pictures into a season book. Discuss different clothing worn for each season and some of the different things that happen in nature during each season.

3. Depending on your geographic locale, ask the children questions about seasonal changes to which they can respond with "some of the time," "most of the time," or "all of the time." Examples are:

   In the spring, does the wind blow some of the time, most of the time, or all of the time?
   In the summer, does the sun shine . . . ?
   In the fall, does the wind blow . . . ?
   In the winter, does it snow . . . ?

Variations/Ways to Extend:

• At various times this week, read a selection from the book of poetry *A Child's Calendar* by John Updike (New York: Knopf, 1965).

• Instead of making a booklet, help the children fold a sheet of paper into quarters and have them draw a picture of a different season in each quadrant.

III-78 PEOPLE MONTAGE

Subject Area: Art

Concepts/Skills: Cuts and pastes
Understands concept of resolutions

Objective: The children will create a montage of magazine pictures of people engaged in constructive activities.

Materials:
- Magazines
- Glue
- Scissors
- Construction paper

Procedure:

1. Provide the children with many magazines and help them find and cut out pictures that depict people exercising, eating well, enjoying themselves, sharing, being considerate and helpful, and so on. Be sure that the pictures stress activities generally regarded as having positive influences on children.

2. Let the children paste the pictures onto paper, overlapping them and filling the paper as a montage. Discuss the idea that the beginning of a new year is a good time to develop some new, good ways of having fun.

Variation/Way to Extend:

- Read the Caldecott Honor book *What Do You Say, Dear? A Book of Manners for All Occasions* by Sesyle Joslin (Reading, MA: Addison-Wesley, 1958). This is a humorous book about manners.

Weekly Subtheme: Getting a Fresh Start

III–79 NEW YEAR PICTURES

Subject Area: Language Arts

Concepts/Skills: Interprets the main idea of a story
Represents thoughts in pictures
Orally labels pictures and drawings

Objectives: The children will listen to a story and show some things they would like to do in this new year by painting with watercolors.

Materials:
- Paper
- Watercolors
- Brushes
- Containers of water
- Book

Procedure:

1. Read *Do You Know What I'll Do?* by Charlotte Zolotow (New York: Harper & Row, 1958) or another book with a similar theme to the children. This one tells of a young girl and her little brother and the girl's ideas about all the wonderful things she would like to do for her brother.

2. Discuss the idea of a new year. Ask the children what sort of things they would like to try doing this year. Some suggestions might be similar to those in the book (doing things for another person) or they might prefer to think of new physical activities (swimming, roller skating, skiing, and so on).

3. Set out the watercolors, containers of water, brushes, and paper and invite the children to paint their own impressions of what was discussed. (If watercolors are unavailable, dilute tempera paint to a light pastel consistency.) You might display these paintings with the caption "In the New Year of _____ , we want to.... "

Variation/Way to Extend:

- Using puppets, demonstrate some desirable ways of behaving for children, such as solving problems by talking and not fighting, cleaning up toys, and helping to put away groceries.

III–80   WINTER IS HERE

Subject Area: Music

Concept/Skill: Claps and marches in time with music

Objectives: The children will learn a new song about winter and clap and march to the rhythm.

Material: • Words and music to "Winter Is Here"

Procedure:

1. Teach the children this simple German folk tune about winter.
2. Let the children sway and move to the music. Also let them clap and march along to the rhythm.

Variation/Way to Extend:

• Let the children use bells to accompany the song.

Winter Is Here

German Folk Tune
Arranged by Kevin DeFreest

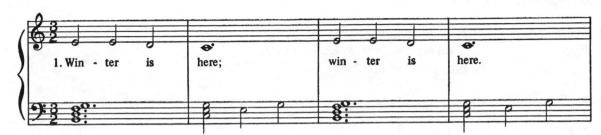

1. Win - ter is here; win - ter is here.

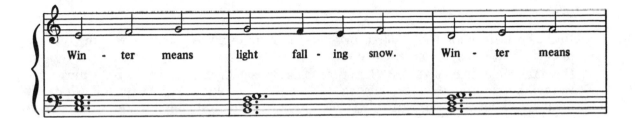

Win - ter means light fall - ing snow. Win - ter means

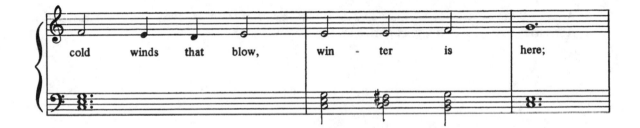

cold winds that blow, win - ter is here;

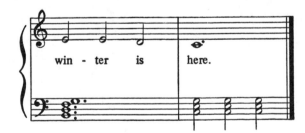

win - ter is here.

2. Winter, goodbye; winter, goodbye.
Leave now, it's time for the spring.
Leave now, let bird voices sing.
Winter, goodbye; winter, goodbye.

© 1986 by The Center for Applied Research in Education, Inc.

Weekly Subtheme: Health and Safety

III–81   EXERCISE FOR HEALTH

Subject Area: Gross Motor Games

Concepts/Skills: Stops movement activity upon command
Claps and marches in time with music
Walks forward and backward

Objective: The children will engage in gross motor activities for fun and exercise.

Materials: • Record player
• Records

Procedure:

1. Begin by instructing the children in some warm-up exercises, such as walking, jumping, hopping, and skipping in a circle to music.
2. Have the children clap and march in time to the music. Each time you stop the music, have the children immediately stop moving. They should be able to produce the following movements: walking backwards, running smoothly, marching, walking heel-to-toe, walking and running on tiptoe, galloping, and skipping.

Variation/Way to Extend:

• An excellent record for this activity is *Movin'* by Hap Palmer, available from Educational Activities, Inc., Box 392, Freeport, NY 11520.

Weekly Subtheme: Health and Safety

III-82   HEALTH CHARADES

Subject Area: Creative Dramatics and Movement

Concepts/Skills: Acts out a familiar story
Cooperates in a group
Listens to directions for activity

Objective: The children will act out scenes depicting healthful ways of behaving.

Materials: • Pictures
• Strips of paper with written or pictured ideas to act out

Procedure:

1. Show pictures of and talk about the basics of good health. Your ideas might include: a child should feel active, have clear skin, good posture, feel refreshed after sleeping, and be able to get along reasonably well with others; we all need to eat nourishing foods from the four basic groups to stay healthy; we all need exercise, rest, and sleep to feel good and stay well; and our bodies need washing and grooming and our teeth need brushing in order to look fit and remain strong.

2. Write out or cut out pictures of these principles on strips of paper. Let those children who want to blindly select one to dramatize. Ask the other children to guess what they are acting out. Examples are: "Pretend you are riding your tricycle for fun and exercise," "Pretend you are brushing your teeth and getting ready for bed," and "Pretend you are eating some delicious, juicy fruit."

Variation/Way to Extend:

• When the children are in the housekeeping area, intervene with reminders of this discussion. You might have the children role play some of the healthful suggestions.

III-83 SAFE OR NOT?

Subject Area: Social Studies

Concepts/Skills: Makes relevant verbal contributions in small group discussion
Works and plays cooperatively with other children
Verbalizes full name and address

Objectives: The children will discuss safety ideas and classify pictures into two groups.

Materials: • Magazine pictures
• Scissors
• Construction paper
• Paste

Procedure:

1. Begin a discussion about safety. Talk about the new toys the children received for the recent holidays and how these items should be used properly. Certain objects (scissors, rubber bands, rope, light sockets, matches, sharp knives, and plastic bags) may not be dangerous in themselves but could be if used by a child or used improperly.
2. Give each child a large sheet of construction paper divided in half with each half labeled "Dangerous" or "Not Dangerous." Have the children find, cut out, and paste in magazine pictures of items or situations that they feel could be dangerous and those that are safe. Let each child talk about the pictures he or she found.

Variations/Ways to Extend:

- Discuss an emergency situation in which a child might have to do the reporting. Display the emergency number for your area (such as 911) and demonstrate calling and reporting the address and nature of the emergency.
- Allow the children to make "tin can telephones" by using empty frozen juice cans with holes punched in the bottoms and the tops cut off. Place six-foot pieces of string through the bottom of the cans and knot them. Let the children practice calling a special number and giving their name, address, and special problem.
- Read *Timmy & the Tin-Can Telephone* by Franklyn M. Branley and Eleanor K. Vaughan (New York: Thomas Y. Crowell, 1959).

III–84 THE CROSSING GUARD SONG

Subject Area: Music

Concept/Skill: Verbalizes a song

Objective: The children will participate in a song about a crossing guard.

Materials:
- Words and music to "The Crossing Guard Song"
- Whistles
- Stop signs

Procedure:

1. Teach "The Crossing Guard Song" to the children. Talk about what a "crossing" is and what a "guard" is. Encourage the children to sing along.
2. This is an action song, so let the children make the suggested motions and sounds with the whistles and stop signs. Let them emphasize the word *stop* with enthusiasm.

Variation/Way to Extend:

- Tape the children singing this song and play it for them, encouraging them to sing along.

The Crossing Guard Song

Words and Music by BOB MESSANO
Arranged by John Sheehan

Allegro (♩ = 100)

1. The cross-ing guard holds up her hand and all the cars must stop *"beep, beep!"*
She waves to me so I can go and all the cars must stop *"beep, beep!"*

Chorus: The cars go beep, beep, beep and she says stop, stop, stop! The

Copyright 1984 Bob Messano

1. The crossing guard blows her whistle
and all the cars must stop!
She waves to me so I can go
and all the cars must stop!
(chorus)

2. The crossing guard holds up a sign
and all the cars must stop!
She waves to me and I can go
and all the cars must stop!
(chorus)

© 1986 by The Center for Applied Research in Education, Inc.

Weekly Subtheme: Health and Safety

III–85 READY FOR WINTER

Subject Areas: Social Studies and Art

Concepts/Skills: Labels common items
Orally labels drawings

Objectives: The children will describe winter activities and understand how to prepare for them.

Materials:
- Paper
- Crayons or markers

Procedure:

1. Make a chart of the following idea: Have the children generate a list of activities and sports that are done outside in winter (ice skating, sled riding, skiing, building snow figures, throwing snowballs, snowmobiling, snowshoeing, ice fishing, traveling by car or foot or plane, shoveling, and so on). Now have them generate a list of clothing and equipment that helps us cope with and enjoy the snow season (coats, hats, ear muffs, mittens, scarves, leg warmers, boots, car chains, salt, ashes, snow plows, and so on).

2. Encourage each child to make a drawing of one of these and dictate a story to you. Emphasize the fun and excitement of winter activities.

Variations/Ways to Extend:

- Read *When Winter Comes* by Charles P. Fox (Wellesley Hills, MA: Lee, 1962). The book contains many black-and-white photographs.
- Invite a professional or amateur winter sport athlete to talk about his or her sport and staying healthy. Choose someone who can actively involve the children in the specialty, such as by bringing ice skates or skis or by showing slides, and so on.

Weekly Subtheme: Snow

III–86 SNOWBALL BOUNCE

Subject Area: Gross Motor Games

Concepts/Skills: Bounces and catches a ball
Rote counts

Objective: The children will play a game bouncing a ball on "snowballs."

Materials:
- Two or three large rubber balls
- Large circles cut from white self-stick vinyl and pressed to the floor

Procedure:

1. Have each child take a turn practicing with a ball. First have them just release it and then push down and release it to learn how to bounce the ball.
2. Tell the children that the white circles on the floor are "snowballs" and that they are going to bounce the ball on the snowballs. After the children have become somewhat accustomed to this, count to see how many times each child can bounce on a "snowball" without losing the ball.

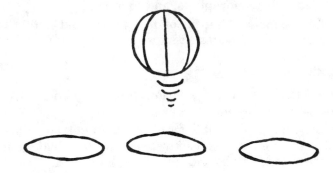

Variations/Ways to Extend:

- Read *A Winter Friend* by Maxine W. Kumin (New York: Putnam, 1961).
- Teach the following fingerplay to the children:

      Five round snowmen (*hold up five fingers*)
      Sitting by the door,
      Out came the sun (*form circle with arms overhead*)
      And there were only four. (*hold up four fingers*)
      Four round snowmen (*hold up four fingers*)
      Sitting by a tree,
      Out came the sun (*form circle with arms overhead*)
      And there were only three. (*hold up three fingers*)
      Three round snowmen (*hold up three fingers*)
      Sitting by the zoo,
      Out came the sun (*form circle with arms overhead*)
      And there were only two. (*hold up two fingers*)
      Two round snowmen (*hold up two fingers*)
      Sitting just for fun,
      Out came the sun (*form circle with arms overhead*)
      And there was only one. (*hold up one finger*)
      One round snowman (*hold up one finger*)
      Wishing he could run,
      Out came the sun (*form circle with arms overhead*)
      And there were none. (*close fist*)

III–87 WHAT'S IN THERE?

Subject Area: Creative Dramatics

Concepts/Skills: Dramatizes a nursery rhyme as teacher recites
Understands prepositions

Objective: The children will interpret and demonstrate the words to a nursery rhyme.

Materials:
- Words to the nursery rhyme
- Props (optional)

Procedure:

1. Read through the accompanying nursery rhyme twice so that the children will be familiar with its content.

What's in there?	The water quenched it
Gold and money.	Where's the water?
Where's my share?	The brown bull drank it.
The mousie's run away with it.	Where's the brown bull?
Where's the mousie?	Behind Burnie's hill.
In her housie.	Where's Burnie's hill?
Where's her housie?	All dressed in snow.
In the woods.	Where's the snow?
Where's the woods?	The sun melted it.
The fire burned it.	Where's the sun?
Where's the fire?	High, high up in the air.

2. Have the children take turns acting out the events or dramatize in groups.

Variations/Ways to Extend:

- If the children express the desire to repeat this rhyme, make a chart with one symbol representing each line. Draw or use cut-out pictures to illustrate.
- For background music this week, play a recording of Debussy's "Snow Is Dancing."

III–88   SNOWFLAKE MOBILE

Subject Area: Art

Concepts/Skills: Develops fine motor movements of folding, cutting, and taping
Pays attention to and concentrates on a task
Explores and discovers

Objective: The children will construct a winter mobile.

Materials:
- Real tree branch or twig for each child
- Scissors
- Shiny white paper circles
- Fishline
- Tape

Procedure:

1. Let each child select a branch to serve as the hanging apparatus of the mobile. Give lengths of fishline to the children and help them loop and tie these around different points of the branch.
2. Distribute the shiny white paper circles and have the children fold each one in half and in half again. Then have them cut designs in these, doily fashion. Encourage the children to make deep cuts along all three sides to add to the snowflake image.
3. Have the children unfold the circles and tape each one to the bottom tip of a piece of hanging fishline. Display the completed mobiles from the ceiling or doorways.

Variations/Ways to Extend:

- Let the children examine real snow with a magnifying glass. Discuss how each and every snowflake is different.
- Read the poem "Snowflakes" by David McCord, found in his book *One at a Time* (Boston: Little, Brown, 1977).

III–89   MELTING SNOW

Subject Area: Science

Concepts/Skills: Observes objects closely
Predicts what will happen next in a situation

Objectives: The children will observe the melting of snow into water and compare the difference in volume.

Materials:
- Snow
- Glass jar
- Tape

Procedure:

1. Discuss the phenomenon of snow. Explain that snow comes from the clouds during winter when the air around the clouds is freezing cold. Snow crystals form from water vapor to grow and fall as snowflakes.
2. Fill a glass jar with snow and mark its volume with a piece of tape. Then allow the snow to melt naturally. Have the children compare the space taken up by the water with the marked amount. (The water takes up much less space because it is the air mixed in with the snowflakes that makes them fluffy.)

Variations/Ways to Extend:

- Experiment with the time it takes for a jar of snow to melt. Try placing it near a heat source or near a cold window. Invite the children to predict what might happen.
- Read the Caldecott Medal book *The Big Snow* by Berta and Elmer Hader (New York: Macmillan, 1948). This is a realistic story about animals' struggle against the elements.

III–90 MARSHMALLOW SNOWMAN SCULPTURE

Subject Area: Nutrition/Foods Experience

Concepts/Skills: Develops fine motor movement of assembling
Describes food by taste

Objective: The children will create marshmallow sculptures.

Materials:
- Large marshmallows
- Toothpicks
- Raisins
- Fruit slices
- Cereal pieces

Procedure:

1. Begin a discussion about building snowmen. Ask the children if they have ever done this.
2. Explain that instead of snow, they are going to use marshmallows to construct snowmen. Give each child three large marshmallows and show the children how to insert the toothpicks so that the marshmallows are aligned vertically. Let them decorate the snowmen with raisins, fruit slices, and cereal pieces to make facial features, a hat, and so on.
3. Have the children disassemble their snowmen and enjoy eating them at snack time. Ask, "How does it taste?"

Variations/Ways to Extend:

- Recite the story *Frosty the Snowman*.
- Teach the accompanying song, "The Land of Colored Snow." Ask the children to imagine snow banks of different-colored snow. Ask, "What would it be like to live in a place with pink or green snow?" "What would your favorite color be for snow?" Make snow cones and use natural fruit juice concentrate to create colored snow.

The Land of Colored Snow

Words and Music by **BOB MESSANO**
Arranged by John Sheehan

© 1986 by The Center for Applied Research in Education, Inc.

Copyright 1984 Bob Messano

III–91   WINTERTIME

Subject Area: Language Arts

Concepts/Skills: Names words that rhyme
Supplies a rhyming word to one given by the teacher

Objectives: The children will listen to a poem about winter and identify the words that rhyme.

Material: • Words to "Wintertime" by Robert Louis Stevenson

Procedure:

1. Read the poem through once just for the children's enjoyment. (Only three of the five verses are given here.)

> WINTERTIME
>
> Close by the jolly fire I sit
> To warm my frozen bones a bit;
> Or with a reindeer sled, explore
> The colder countries 'round the door.
>
> When to go out, my nurse doth wrap
> Me in my comforter and cap;
> The cold wind burns my face and blows
> Its frosty pepper up my nose.
>
> Black are my steps on silver sod
> Thick blow my frosty breath
> And tree and house, and hill and lake,
> Are frosted like a wedding cake.

2. Then instruct the children to listen for words that rhyme in the poem (demonstrate rhyming words first, if necessary), and to tell which ones they are. Then repeat the words that rhyme and ask the children to think of some more, such as *sit/bit/hit/mitt*; *wrap/cap/map/tap*; and so on.

Variation/Way to Extend:

• Listen to a recording of "Waltz on the Ice" by Prokofieff as background music while the children paint with thick white tempera on blue paper.

III–92 ICICLES

Subject Area: Gross Motor Games

Concepts/Skills: Catches a ball with hands only
Throws a ball with direction
Throws a ball in the air and catches it by self

Objective: The children will play a game of catch with a ball.

Material: • Large soft ball

Procedure:

1. Have the children stand in a row opposite you and pretend to be straight icicles. Call out "Icicle" and the name of a child before you throw the ball to that child (for example, "Icicle Meredith"). Tell each child to try to catch the ball using only his or her hands and then throw it back to you.
2. Play the game again, this time allowing each child to throw the ball in the air and to try to catch it by him- or herself.

Variations/Ways to Extend:

- Try this activity first with a large ball and then a considerably smaller one to increase the skill.
- Obtain an 11″ × 14″ art reproduction of "A Scene on the Ice" by Hendrick Avercamp (No. 2315) from the National Gallery of Art, Publications Service, Washington, DC 20565. Be sure to write for a catalog and prices.

III-93   WATER HAS WEIGHT

Subject Area: Science

Concepts/Skills: Predicts what will happen next in a situation
Observes objects closely
Pays attention and concentrates on a task

Objective: The children will observe that when water is added to a material, the material becomes heavier.

Materials: • Inexpensive postage scale
• Paper cups
• Oaktag
• Marker
• Sand
• Water
• Pebbles

Procedure:

1. Introduce the scale to the children and discuss the concept of determining weight. Allow the children to hold light and heavy objects; then weigh each object on the scale and announce its weight in ounces

2. Show the children an empty paper cup and ask if it is light or heavy. Place the paper cup on the scale, note its weight, and ask, "What will happen if we pour some water into the cup?" Show how the scale's pointer moves down after the water is poured. Then ask, "Which cup is heavier, the empty one or the one with water in it?" Emphasize the fact that water has weight—it can make an empty cup heavier.

3. Now pour two equal portions of sand (about two ounces each) into two dry cups. Using the scale, show the children that both cups are equal in weight. Ask, "What will happen if we pour some water into one of the cups of sand?" Proceed to pour one ounce of water into the cup. Compare the weights and point out that water has weight even though it has been absorbed by the sand.

4. Repeat the procedure using pebbles instead of sand. On oaktag, create bar graphs representing the weights of the dry and wet materials.

Variations/Ways to Extend:

• Discuss and demonstrate some of the water experiments described in *Let's Try It Out: Wet & Dry* by Seymour Simon (New York: McGraw-Hill, 1969).
• Experiment with other materials, such as dirt and leaves. Weigh them dry, then wet.

III-94 FOOD COLOR SPLASH

Subject Area: Art

Concepts/Skills: Makes choices
Explores and discovers

Objective: The children will create original designs with food coloring and water.

Materials:
- Bottles of food coloring
- Jars of water
- White paper towels
- White typing paper
- Newsprint
- Brushes

Procedure:

1. Allow the children some creative experimenting with the sharp colors that drops of food coloring produce on paper towels versus the mixture they will get by diluting food coloring with water and painting on paper. For the former, have the children fold the paper towels into quarters and drop splashes of different colors onto the towel. Open the towel to see the lovely spreading effect.

2. Then have the children dip their brushes into diluted food coloring and paint first on newsprint and then on white typing paper. Talk about the results, comparing the three types of effects produced.

Variation/Way to Extend:

- Read *The Sky Was Blue* by Charlotte Zolotow (New York: Harper & Row, 1963).

III–95 FLOAT OR SINK?

Subject Area: Science and Math

Concepts/Skills: Predicts outcome of experiment

Understands that some things float and some things sink in water

Objectives: The children will observe, record, hypothesize, test, and compare in a water experiment.

Materials:
- Pan of water
- Objects (rocks, toys, clips, corks, paper, balls, bottle caps, and so on)
- Oaktag
- Marker
- Glue (optional)
- Pictures of objects used (optional)

Procedure:

1. Ask the children to predict whether each object will sink or float in a pan of water.
2. Make a chart showing the actual results. Use pictures or drawings of the objects used to place on the chart, or glue the actual objects onto the oaktag.

3. Allow the children to play with the objects, experimenting with their properties in water.

Variation/Way to Extend:

- Read *The Story About Ping* by Marjorie Flack (New York: Penguin, 1977).

TRANSPORTATION

- ○ By Land
- ○ By Rail
- ○ By Water
- ○ By Air

III-96   WAYS TO GET AROUND

Subject Areas: Language Arts and Art

Concepts/Skills: Describes a familiar object and knows its use
Classifies objects
Makes a simple comparison of two objects in terms of difference

Objectives: The children will talk about and examine pictures of different land transportation methods and vehicles and construct a collage.

Materials:
- Chart paper
- Pictures of land transportation methods or vehicles
- Markers
- Clear self-stick vinyl
- Oaktag
- Glue

Procedure:

1. Start a discussion about transportation, including who and what are transported and why. Let the children generate a list of ways we move around on land (via cars, trucks, buses, bicycles, skates, motorcycles, feet, skis, wagons, carts, horses, elephants, dogs, and so on) and record this on chart paper. Show pictures of each one.
2. Sort and compare those that require motors with those that do not. Sort and compare those that use wheels with those that do not. Discuss which move people, food, clothing, and supplies.
3. Let the children make a group collage by pasting all the pictures onto oaktag. Cover the collage with clear self-stick vinyl.

Variation/Way to Extend:

- Play a thinking game. Make up a list of statements describing modes of land transportation and have the children guess the vehicle or method. Here are two examples:

    I have four wheels and children put toys in me. I am a _____ . (wagon)
    I am worn on the feet to slide down a mountain of snow. I am _____ . (skis)

III-97   TRANSPORTATION SETS

Subject Area: Math

Concept/Skill: Identifies a set as a collection of objects having a common property

Objective: The children will classify paper shapes into sets by recognizing similarities.

Materials: • Paper cut-outs of cars, trucks, buses, horses, elephants, tricycles, wagons, and so on
• Glue
• Large sheet of oaktag divided into six sections for each child

Procedure:

1. Discuss the idea that a set is a collection of objects that all have at least one characteristic that is the same.
2. Have enough land transportation cut-outs so that each child can have at least three of each item in each section of his or her paper.
3. Mix the shapes together and distribute them to the children. Ask each child to sort and glue one set in each section of the paper.

Variations/Ways to Extend:

• If your class size is too large for the number of paper cut-outs needed, use commercial stickers instead.
• Read *The Big Book of Real Trucks* by Elizabeth Cameron (New York: Grosset & Dunlap, 1970).
• Let the children have fun sorting and making sets using a big box of various buttons. These can be sorted by size, shape, color, number of holes, or type (military, babies', ladies', and so on).

Weekly Subtheme: By Land

III–98 TRANSPORTATION PROP BOX

Subject Area: Creative Dramatics and Movement

Concepts/Skills: Becomes self-aware
Works and plays cooperatively with other children
Understands the concept of sequence

Objective: The children will use props to help them act out transportation situations.

Materials: • Prop box containing transportation items
• Ideas for dramatizing

Procedure:

1. Fill a prop box with many items (uniforms, hats, tickets, change makers, helmets, and so on) used by people who work with land vehicles.
2. Allow the children to dress up and play the various parts of bus driver, truck driver, motorcycle police officer, ambulance driver, race car driver, chauffeur, mechanic, and service station attendant. Let one or two children begin the activity and slowly have the others join the action. Supply the children with a basic idea, such as the truck driver needs directions, have all the other characters offer their own advice, and let the action proceed from there.

Variations/Ways to Extend:

• Read *All Around the Town* by Phyllis McGinley (Philadelphia: Lippincott, 1948).
• Invite persons who work at some of the jobs mentioned here to visit the classroom. Ask them to bring in items related to the job that the children can handle.
• Obtain attractive posters from the American Automobile Association (AAA), Traffic Safety and Education, 8111 Gatehouse Road, Falls Church, VA 22042.

III-99 PARTS OF A CAR

Subject Area: Science

Concepts/Skills: Inquires and explores
Solves problems

Objectives: The children will talk about the workings of a car and construct a "mechanical" object with woodworking materials and tools.

Materials:
- Pictures of cars
- Plastic models of car engines
- Smooth wood scraps
- Woodworking tools
- Small mechanical pieces

Procedure:

1. Begin a circle talk about the parts of a car and how these parts are similar to those of buses and trucks. Show pictures of cars and let the children generate a list of what they know about interior and exterior parts. Then display plastic models of car engines that show carburetor, piston action, and so on.

2. Give the children lots of screws, nuts, bolts, chains, rubber washers, and so on and let them feel and discuss these mechanical parts. Then set up a woodworking activity with small tools and wood scraps and let the children combine and construct from all of these materials.

Variation/Way to Extend:

- Show two filmstrips, "Off We Go" and "Rolling Along," from the Fundamentals of Science series published by Eye Gate Media, Inc., 146-01 Archer Avenue, Jamaica, NY 11435.

III–100   MILK CARTON VEHICLES

Subject Area: Art

Concepts/Skills: Makes choices and explores
                         Develops eye–hand coordination

Objectives: The children will construct four-wheeled vehicles and paint them.

Materials:
- Milk cartons
- Construction paper circles
- Yarn
- Name tags
- Tempera paints
- Brushes
- Paper fasteners
- Glue
- Tape

Procedure:

1. Discuss the idea of how a wheel makes it possible to move heavy loads easily and makes it possible for many types of vehicles to move.
2. Let the children decide what type of vehicle they would like to make out of the milk carton and paint appropriately. For example, a red milk carton might be a fire engine; yellow, a taxi; white, an ambulance or police car; or black, a truck. Mix a little glue with each child's color choice to make the paint adhere to the waxy surface of the milk carton.
3. When the paint is dry, attach paper fasteners through the paper circles and then through the carton for wheels. Tape yarn to the front of the vehicles so that the children can pull them. You might also have the children tape name tags and the names of the make of the vehicles to the sides for identification.

Variation/Way to Extend:
- Read *The Great Big Car & Truck Book* by Richard Scarry (Racine, WI: Western, 1951).

III–101 RAILROAD MUSIC

Subject Area: Music

Concepts/Skills: Responds rhythmically
Claps and marches to music

Objectives: The children will appreciate and move to some music about trains.

Materials:
- Small train set
- Record player
- Musical recordings about trains

Procedure:

1. Let the children play with a small train set and note the action of the wheels.
2. Play some recordings that portray the rhythm and mood of a train ride. Two good selections are on Ella Jenkins' album *Seasons for Singing*, available from Folkways Records, 632 Broadway, New York, NY 10012. "This Train" and "Freight Train Blues" provide high action and good rhythm to move to with enthusiasm.
3. Once the children have recognized the rhythm, have them clap to it. Then have them form a line. Instruct them to bend their arms at their elbows and move them forward in circles, imitating the wheels of a train. Circle around the room, moving to the music and chugging and whistling along.

Variation/Way to Extend:

- Read *The Little Train* by Lois Lenski (New York: Walck, 1940).

III–102   NUMBER TRAIN

Subject Area: Math

Concepts/Skills: Understands ordinal positions, first through fifth
Develops fine motor movements of tracing, cutting, and pasting

Objective: The children will construct a paper train that demonstrates ordinal positions.

Materials:
- Cardboard
- Markers
- Paste
- 11″ × 14″ sheets of construction paper
- Railroad shapes (see patterns)

Procedure:

1. Prepare several cardboard cutouts of railroad engines and cars. Help the children trace a train onto large sheets of construction paper.
2. Write the numerals *1, 2, 3, 4, 5* on each car and the words *first, second, third, fourth, fifth* on each, respectively.
3. Have the children try to arrange the railroad cars in order on another sheet of paper and paste them in place when they are correctly laid out. Encourage verbalization of the names of the ordinal positions while the children work.

Variation/Way to Extend:

- Use this activity to reinforce counting as well. Let the children imagine a very long train and ask, "How many cars can you count?"

© 1986 by The Center for Applied Research in Education, Inc.

III–103 TRAIN POETRY

Subject Area: Language Arts

Concepts/Skills: Names two words that rhyme
Listens to stories and poems

Objective: The children will listen to a poem about trains.

Materials: • Words to "From a Railway Carriage" by Robert Louis Stevenson
• Easel paints (optional)
• Situations to dramatize (optional)

Procedure:

1. Read the following lyrical poem to the children, pointing out to them how the words have the rhythm and speed feeling of a train. Let the children identify rhyming words, with help if necessary.

FROM A RAILWAY CARRIAGE

Faster than fairies, faster than witches,
Bridges and houses, hedges and ditches;
And charging along like troops in a battle,
All through the meadows the horses and cattle;
All of the sights of the hill and the plain
Fly as thick as driving rain;
And ever again in the wink of an eye,
Painted stations whistle by.

2. Use the poem as a stimulus for easel paintings or situations to dramatize.

Variations/Ways to Extend:

• Make poetry time special by allowing the children to be as comfortable and relaxed as possible. Concentrate on the beauty and feeling of the poems.
• After the children have had a chance to enjoy the sheer power of the words, help them to get the meanings of the words they might not understand and then have them listen to the poem again with increased understanding.

III–104 TRAIN PRINT

Subject Area: Art

Concept/Skill: Explores mixed media

Objective: The children will create prints to represent a train.

Materials:
- Tempera paints
- Shallow containers
- Rectangular sponges
- Newsprint
- Paper towels
- Yarn
- Newspapers
- Black marker

Procedure:

1. Use newspapers to cover the table and to provide a cushion for printing.
2. Place a few sheets of paper towels in containers and pour in tempera paints to create a printing pad. Press a sponge onto the pad and print a train design onto the newsprint. Explain to the children that these sponge rectangles represent the cars of a train. Tell the children that they may line up their sponge prints in a line or curve or however else they wish to picture a train.
3. When the prints are dry, let the children glue the yarn in place to connect the cars and make a train. Have the children use black markers to draw wheels and tracks beneath the trains. Help each child make the front car resemble an engine and the final car, a caboose.

Variation/Way to Extend:

- Plan to visit a train station and, if possible, take a train ride. If you cannot arrange this type of trip, invite an engineer or conductor to talk with your class.

III–105   ALL ABOARD!

Subject Area: Creative Dramatics and Movement

Concepts/Skills: Participates in imaginative play
Responds to nondirective questions
Proposes alternate ways of doing something

Objective: The children will demonstrate role playing of passengers and conductors on a train.

Materials:
• Props for passengers (newspapers, doll, glasses, jackets, tickets, and so on)
• Props for conductor (hat, ticket puncher, whistle, and so on)
• Chairs arranged like seats in a train car

Procedure:

1. Select a small group of children to be passengers and provide them with the props listed here. Explain that they are waiting at a train station to board a train when it arrives. Suggest that some of the passengers are tired of waiting (they check their watches or they pace around). Describe weather conditions (it's getting windy or cold, it's starting to rain).

2. When the train finally arrives, have the conductor yell out, "All aboard! Tickets, please!" Encourage the children to talk to one another and to the conductor as they board the train and take a seat while the conductor punches their tickets. Make nondirective statements to the children, such as, "You're really enjoying this train ride." When appropriate, ask such questions as "Will you allow a passenger on if he or she has no ticket?"

3. Encourage as many children as possible to participate. Provide props for more than one conductor.

Variation/Way to Extend:

• Create problem situations for the children to deal with, such as a temperamental passenger who insists on having a seat by the window or a passenger who wants to get off the train in between stations. Encourage the children to find their own solutions.

Weekly Subtheme: By Water

III–106 BOAT BOOK

Subject Areas: Social Studies and Language Arts

Concepts/Skills: Develops fine motor movements of cutting and pasting
Orally labels pictures

Objective: The children will construct a boat book.

Materials:
- Vacation and/or nautical magazines
- Construction paper
- Scissors
- Paste
- Yarn
- Hole puncher
- Crayons or markers (optional)

Procedure:

1. Start a discussion with the children about the many types of boats that exist. Talk about the different uses each has and about the various ways they are powered (wind, rowing, outboard or inboard motor, and steam).
2. Look through the magazines together and have the children cut out pictures of boats or that are related to boats and have them paste these sheets on construction paper that have been cut in the shape of a boat.

3. Punch two holes along one side of each sheet and tie the pages together with yarn. You might also want the children to draw boat pictures in these books and dictate words for you to record in them.

Variations/Ways to Extend:

- Read *Boats on the River* by Marjorie Flack (New York: Viking Press, 1946).
- For background music this week, play "Boating on the Lake" by Kullak.

III-107   PLAY BOAT

Subject Areas: Art and Creative Dramatics

Concepts/Skills: Acts out a familiar story as teacher recites
Works and plays cooperatively with others

Objectives: The children will construct a boat from a box and use it to engage in dramatic play.

Materials:
- Very large cardboard box
- Paints
- Brushes
- Sailor caps
- Utility knife
- Boat props (what kind depends on what type of boat is made—see "Procedure")

Procedure:

1. Cut off one entire side of a large cardboard box positioned horizontally. Let the children paint it and decorate it as a boat or large ship. If they choose to fashion a sailboat, provide a stick attached to a large sheet and help them tape this to the inside front of the box. For a rowboat, provide small brooms for oars or cut out cardboard oars. An ocean liner may have port holes painted along the sides.

2. After the boat is complete and dry, use it as a prop for a stimulating creative dramatics experience. Selecting a scene from a book familiar to the children often results in a successful experience; however, a spontaneous creative experience can also be had when you present a problem to the children and guide their reactions. For example, suggest to two or three children that they are sailors out in the boat on a hot day. Ask, "How will you keep yourselves cool?" Many situations can be described as long as they are short, uncomplicated, and appropriate to the experience of the children.

Variation/Way to Extend:

- In advance, prepare index cards containing ideas for role playing. Then let small groups of children select which situation they would like to role play.

III-108   SAILOR GAMES

Subject Area: Gross Motor Games

Concept/Skill: Develops balance by walking an eight-foot line, hopping on each foot four times, and standing on each foot for five seconds

Objective: The children will play body coordination games with a sailor theme.

Materials:
- 12″ × 18″ sheet of white construction paper for each child
- Stapler
- Material needed for the games (see "Procedure")
- Marker

Procedure:

1. Help the children fold the paper in half so that the two 12″ sides meet. Next, have them fold a flap by taking the bottom edge of the paper facing them and folding it up to the top edge. Have the children turn the paper over and do the same on the other side. Write the word *sailor* across the front and staple the sides together.

2. While the children are wearing their caps, have them engage in sailor games:

   Walk the Plank—Use masking tape to tape an eight-foot line on the floor in an open area. Have the children practice walking back and forth without stepping off, putting one foot in front of the other. Then try it heel-to-toe, then backwards.
   Sailor Hop—Have the children hop four times on the right foot and then four times on the left foot. For a sailor "look," have them shade their eyes with their hands while hopping.
   Land Ahoy—Ask each child to balance on his or her right foot and shade the eyes while you yell, "Land ahoy" and count to five. Have them do the same with the left foot. Tell the children that they are pretending to look for land from their ships.

Variation/Way to Extend:

- Use instrumental music with a nautical feeling to accompany these games.

III–109 PICTURE POEM

Subject Area: Language Arts

Concepts/Skills: Develops creativity
Describes a scene with several statements
Listens to directions

Objective: The children will create a poem about a boat.

Materials: • Pictures and photographs of boats
• 11″ × 14″ sheets of art paper
• Marker

Procedure:

1. Discuss with the children the idea of a boat and the many types that exist (rowboats, canoes, motor boats, submarines, ocean liners, tugboats, ferries, houseboats, and sailboats). Use pictures and photographs of these various boats to help the children understand.

2. On a one-to-one basis with each child, try to elicit a poem following these steps:

   Ask the child to think about one of the kinds of boats discussed earlier.

   Ask the child to give you two words that tell how the boat looks in his or her mind. Record the words.

   Ask the child what is happening to the boat or what it is doing. Record three of the child's answers.

   Ask what the child thinks about the boat. Record a phrase or an idea.

   Ask the child to give you one word that means the same thing as "boat." Record this as the end of the poem.

3. Read to the child what you have written. Tell the child that it is a beautiful poem and that you would like one word as a title or name. Record this above the poem.

4. The results should be wonderful and surprisingly poetic, as shown in this example by a four-year-old:

   A Houseboat
   Motor, fishing line,
   Sailing, turning, tipping,
   A boat like a house that can sail across the ocean.
   A ship.

5. Display the poems at the children's eye-level.

Variation/Way to Extend:

• If the words are written for the child on art paper that is large enough, have the child draw an illustration of the poem for a wonderful picture poem.

III–110   MICHAEL, ROW THE BOAT ASHORE

Subject Area: Music

Concepts/Skills: Performs
Develops creativity
Claps and sways in time to music

Objective: The children will learn a folk song about boating.

Material: • Words and music to "Michael, Row the Boat Ashore"

Procedure:

1. Teach the American folk song (found on the next page) about a man and his rowboat. Let the children clap and sway to the tune.
2. After the children are comfortable with the melody, let them substitute one another's name for "Michael." Also encourage the children to think about other aspects of boating that they would like to express in the song. Create new lyrics for these ideas, such as:

   Susan's boat is going slow . . .
   Jimmy's canoe is shiny and new . . .

Variation/Way to Extend:

• Invite a parent or other visitor to bring the class a small aluminum boat, a ship in the bottle, or other model for the children to examine.

Michael Row the Boat Ashore

Folk Song from Georgia
Arranged by Kevin DeFreest

2. Pull the boat through waters deep, Alleluia!
   Pull the boat through waters deep, Alleluia!

3. Michael's boat is made of wood, Alleluia!
   Michael's boat is made of wood, Alleluia!

© 1986 by The Center for Applied Research in Education, Inc.

III–111 PAPER AIRPLANES

Subject Area: Science

Concepts/Skills: Solves problems
Develops fine motor movement of folding
Tests

Objectives: The children will construct paper airplanes and make them fly.

Materials: • 8½″ × 11″ sheets of paper
• Markers or crayons

Procedure:

1. Help the children fold the paper according to the following steps:

   Hold the paper vertically. Fold down the left corner, with the point at center.
   Fold down the right corner to create a point at the top of the paper.
   Fold the paper in half vertically, toward self.
   Fold the sides back into wings and fold down 1″ flaps.

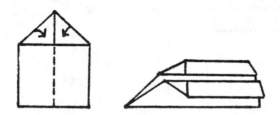

2. Have the children color their airplanes and practice making them fly.

Variation/Way to Extend:

• Read *Let's Take an Airplane Trip* by Billy N. Pope (San Angelo, TX: Taylor Publishing, 1975).

Weekly Subtheme: By Air

III–112 AIRPLANE AND HANGAR

Subject Area: Math

Concept/Skill: Understands one-to-one correspondence by matching members of equivalent sets

Objective: The children will match sets of airplane hangars and airplanes.

Materials: • Sheet of paper for each child with six hangars drawn on
 • Six small paper airplane cut-outs for each child
 • Glue

Procedure:

1. Give each child a sheet of paper with six hangars drawn on it. Explain that a hangar is to an airplane what a garage is to a car. Then give each child six small paper airplane cut-outs.

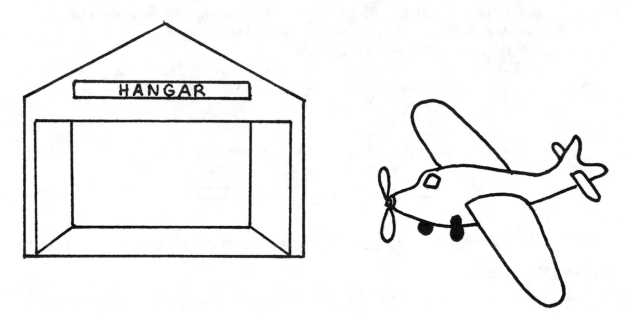

2. Ask the children to paste one airplane in front of each hangar. (The children are matching a set of airplanes to a set of hangars.)

Variation/Way to Extend:

• Read *Ann Can Fly* by Frederick Phleger (New York: Beginner Books, 1959).

III–113   ROCKET SHIPS

Subject Area: Art

Concepts/Skills: Explores
                       Uses new materials

Objective: The children will construct rocket ships in launching pads.

Materials:
- Cardboard tubes
- Aluminum foil
- Brushes
- Styrofoam circular bases
- Waterbase metallic silver paint

Procedure:

1. Have the children paint the styrofoam circular bases with the silver paint. When dry, these will serve as the launching pads.
2. Now have the children wrap their cardboard tubes with aluminum foil. Let them crumble a small amount of foil to shape into a cone and stuff into the top of the rocket body.
3. Press the cardboard tube into the styrofoam to finish the project.

Variations/Ways to Extend:

- Read *When I Go to the Moon* by Claudia Lewis (New York: Macmillan, 1961).
- Let the children make lovely outer-space paintings with watercolors. Moons, stars, the sun, planets, and rocket ships can easily be represented by the children.

III-114   BLAST OFF!

Subject Area: Creative Dramatics and Movement

Concepts/Skills: Develops creativity
Role plays
Cooperates in a group

Objective: The children will dramatize an outer-space situation.

Materials:
- Large box
- Paints
- Brushes
- Paper bags
- Scissors
- Tools
- Telephones
- Pads
- Pencils

Procedure:

1. Obtain a very large box and have the children paint and decorate it as a rocket ship. Stand the box vertically and cut a door in it.
2. Let the children choose roles to play, such as those of astronauts, ground crew, and control center personnel. Give the astronauts paper bag helmets with face holes cut out; the ground crew, some dull (not sharp) tools from the woodworking center; and the control center group, telephones, pads, and pencils.
3. Lay out a framework of a situation for the children and have them enact it. Begin with a good exercise in rote counting backwards: "10-9-8-7-6-5-4-3-2-1—BLAST OFF!" Some sample situations are:

   You are in space. There is no gravity. You are happily floating around. Have control center give you advice.

   You have landed on another plant. What do you find? What do you bring back to Earth? How will the ground crew help you unload your precious cargo?

Variations/Ways to Extend:

- At snack time, provide instant citrus drinks and breakfast bars. Discuss why these types of products were developed for traveling in space.
- For information on the history of space flight, planets, space food, photographs, and a film catalog, write to Educator's Media Resources Library, Mail Code ERL, Kennedy Space Center, FL 32899. Ask for the free Teacher's Kit.

Weekly Subtheme: By Air

III–115   HERE'S A LITTLE AIRPLANE

Subject Area: Language Arts

Concept/Skill: Verbalizes a fingerplay

Objectives: The children will listen to and act out a fingerplay about airplanes.

Material: • Words to the fingerplay

Procedure:

1. Teach the following fingerplay to the children:

> Here's a little airplane (*cross index fingers*)
> Zooming way up high,
> Here's the bright and shining sun (*make circle with hands*)
> Watching it go by.
> Here's the big, black puffy clouds (*hold hands flat*)
> Dripping drops of rain, (*wave fingers*)
> Here's the thunder clapping (*clap loudly*)
> With all its might and main!
> Here's a little airplane (*cross index fingers*)
> Coming from the sky,
> Into its cozy hangar (*cup hand*)
> Where it will be nice and dry.

2. Help the children memorize the first four lines of the fingerplay.

Variation/Way to Extend:

• Try to visit an airport to give the children a rich experience. If this is not possible, invite a pilot, controller, or flight attendant to talk with the children.

ANIMALS

- ○ Forest Animals
- ○ Pets
- ○ Zoo Animals
- ○ The Circus and Circus Animals

III-116   FOREST ANIMAL BOOK

Subject Area: Language Arts

Concepts/Skills: Labels common items (animals)
Makes relevant verbal contribution in small group discussion
Uses more than one attribute to describe

Objectives: The children will discuss, identify, and cut out pictures of animals to form a book.

Materials:
- Construction paper
- Scissors
- Yarn
- Magazines and other sources of animal pictures
- Markers
- Glue
- Hole puncher

Procedure:

1. Begin with a discussion of forest animals, including deer, foxes, oppossum, rabbits, raccoons, skunks, bears, squirrels, turtles, chipmunks, and birds. See how many of each animal's attributes the children can list.

2. Explain to the children that each day this week they will look for pictures of these animals to paste onto paper and form a book. Label the pictures for the children and add some of their descriptive terms to each page.

Variation/Way to Extend:

- Read one or two of Aesop's Fables to the children. "The Hare and the Tortoise" and "The Grasshopper and the Ants" are two well-known favorites.

III-117   MORE BIRDS OR WORMS?

Subject Area: Math

Concept/Skill: Distinguishes between equivalent and non-equivalent sets through matching

Objective: The children will work with felt figures of birds and worms to match sets.

Materials:
- Rectangle of flannel for each child
- Cardboard for each child
- Scissors
- Felt shapes (see patterns)
- Glue
- Stapler
- Shirt boxes (optional)

Procedure:

1. Make an individual flannelboard for each child by stapling a rectangle of heavy, fuzzy flannel to a piece of cardboard (or staple to the top of a cardboard shirt box for a flannelboard with its own storage space for felt cutouts).
2. Use the patterns to cut out enough simple worm shapes and bird shapes from felt so that each child has five of each with which to work.
3. Have each child line up the worms and the birds at the bottom of the flannelboard. Talk about the two *sets,* matching one in each set to one in the other. Explain that they have the same number, so they are *equivalent* sets.
4. Tell a story wherein a bird eats a worm (take one worm away). Now the two sets do not match because they do not have the same number of members. They are *non-equivalent* sets. Have a bird eat another worm and compare again. Try having one or two birds fly away and ask the children if the sets are equivalent or non-equivalent.

Variation/Way to Extend:

- Use these cut-outs for counting, matching, one-to-one correspondence, and comparing more or less. Later use them for adding and subtracting, such as "4 birds and 1 bird are 5 birds," or "3 worms take away 1 worm leaves 2 worms."

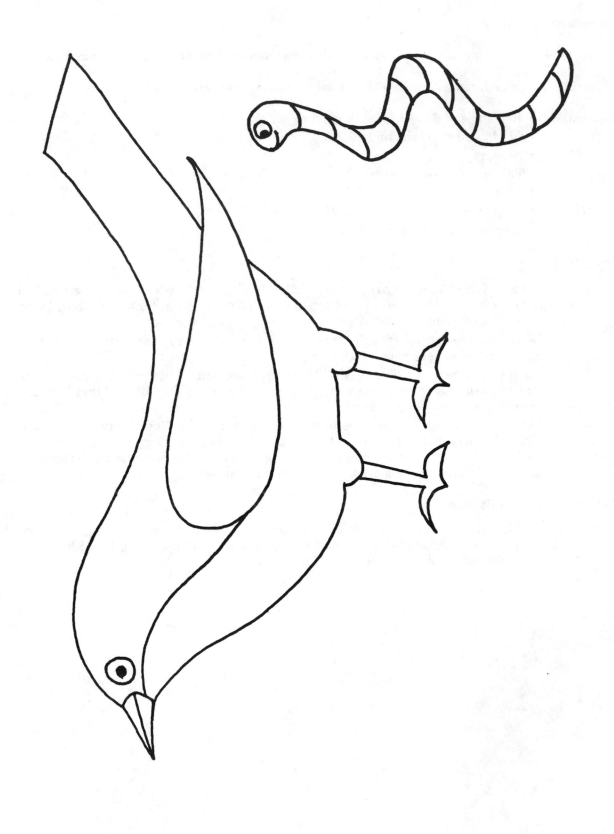

© 1986 by The Center for Applied Research in Education, Inc.

III-118 TURTLE MOSAIC

Subject Area: Art

Concepts/Skills: Handles new materials
Controls a brush and paint
Pastes

Objectives: The children will construct a turtle and decorate it with eggshell pieces.

Materials:
- Small paper plates
- Glue
- Scissors
- Green paint
- Brushes
- Hard-boiled eggs
- Food coloring
- Black paper
- White vinegar
- Containers of warm water

Procedure:

1. Dye the hard-boiled eggs by dipping each one into mixtures of warm water, vinegar, and food coloring. Allow the colored eggs to dry and cool before peeling and crumbling the shells. (Use the insides for egg salad on crackers at snack time.) Set the crumbled eggshells aside.

2. Have each child use green paint to color the back side of a paper plate. Then have the child cut five oval shapes from black paper and paste them onto the plate as the turtle's head and four feet.

3. Help the children paste the different-colored shell pieces onto the turtles' backs for a multi-colored shell effect.

Variation/Way to Extend:

- On the unpainted side of the turtle, paste a copy of a poem for each child. A good selection is "The Little Turtle" by Vachel Lindsay, found in her *Collected Poems,* rev. ed. (New York: Macmillan, 1925).

III-119 CONNECT-THE-DOTS ANIMAL

Subject Area: Art

Concept/Skill: Develops fine motor movement of connecting a dotted outline to make a shape

Objective: The children will complete a picture of an animal by connecting the dots with a crayon.

Materials:
- Crayons
- Paper
- Dot-to-dot animal
- Photocopier, mimeograph machine, or other reproducing equipment

Procedure:

1. Using whatever copying equipment is available, make a copy of the dot-to-dot animal for each child.
2. Tell the children to use a crayon to connect the dots and complete the picture.

Variation/Way to Extend:

- Invite a bird watcher, ranger, park director, or naturalist to visit the class. Before the visit, have the children role play what they expect the person's job to be about. Later, discuss with the children how realistic their expectations were.

© 1986 by The Center for Applied Research in Education, Inc.

III-120   CASTING ANIMAL TRACKS

Subject Area: Science

Concepts/Skills: Observes
Records
Relates

Objectives: The children will locate, describe, and compare animal tracks and create casts of what they find.

Materials: • Large outdoor area
• Small milk cartons with tops and bottoms removed
• Plaster of Paris, mixed and ready to pour

Procedure:

1. Explain to the children that animals leave their tracks in mud, snow, and sand. In a large outdoor area, help the children look for distinctive tracks (made from toes, hoofs, nails, claws, and heels) left in the mud. By noting the direction of the toes, you can tell in which directions the animal was going. Explain that some animals travel on their toes, some on their toenails, and some on heels and toes; some hop, and some jump along.

2. When you and the children find some tracks, make a cast by placing the open milk carton over the track and pouring the mixture of plaster of Paris into the carton. Wait until it sets; then lift to see the tracks you have imprinted.

3. Some of the children may want to identify the animal source of the tracks. Check with the National Audubon Society, 950 Third Avenue, New York, NY 10022 (212-832-3200) or the National Wildlife Federation, 1412 16th Street N.W., Washington, DC 20036, for books and charts depicting animals with their tracks.

Variations/Ways to Extend:

• Add dry powdered tempera to the plaster of Paris mixture for colorful casts of animal tracks.
• Read *Some of Us Walk, Some Fly, Some Swim* by Michael Frith (New York: Beginner Books, 1971).

III-121 PET CHART

Subject Areas: Social Studies and Language Arts

Concepts/Skills: Speaks in sentences of six or more words
Makes relevant verbal contribution to discussion
Shows an interest in the printed word
Describes a simple object using the criteria of color, size, shape, composition, and use

Objective: The children will contribute to a chart showing information about their pets.

Materials:
- Pictures
- Large sheet of chart paper
- Marker

Procedure:

1. Show pictures of common household pets and begin a discussion about pets, including dogs, cats, birds, fish, hamsters, guinea pigs, gerbils, and turtles. Talk about the pets owned by the children. Explain that just about any tame animal kept for enjoyment and companionship can be considered a pet, although the ones listed here are the most common household pets. Talk about how pets need food, water, shelter, and loving care.

2. Make a large classroom chart entitled "Our Pets." Ask the children who have pets to contribute information for the chart. Have columns labeled "Child's Name," "Pet Type," "Pet's Name," and "Description of the Pet." A sample chart is shown here.

Our Pets

Child's Name	Pet Type	Pet's Name	Description of the Pet
Keith	fish	Spotty	Orange and swims fast
Amy	gerbil	Furry	Eats lettuce from my hand
Patrick	dog	Jasper	Big and noisy

Variations/Ways to Extend:

- Before this lesson, send home a note with each child asking for a picture of the family pet(s), if any. Use the pictures in addition to the words in the column "Pet Type."
- Let the children who do not have a pet at home choose a picture of a pet they would like to have. Add their information to the chart.
- Read *Animals Every Child Should Know* by Dena Humphreys (New York: Grosset & Dunlap, 1962).

Weekly Subtheme: Pets

III-122 CLASSROOM PET

Subject Area: Science

Concepts/Skills: Understands that each animal needs its own kind of food and shelter
Observes objects closely
Shows an increasing curiosity

Objectives: The children will observe a pet in the classroom and describe its requirements for care.

Materials:
- Borrowed pet or aquarium of fish
- Large sheet of chart paper
- Cut-out pictures or crayons
- Glue

Procedure:

1. Arrange to have a suitable pet remain in the classroom for this week of discovery. If that is not possible, start a small aquarium of a few fish.
2. Encourage the children to observe the characteristics and needs of the pet. Note the pet's covering, mouth, method of movement, color, sound, and sleeping and eating habits. Ask, "What exercise does it need?" "How does it protect itself?" "What kind of habitat does it need?" "How does it reproduce?"
3. Make a chart of these categories and assist the children in finding the answers. Use pictures on the chart to show what was found out.

Variations/Ways to Extend:

- Ask a veterinarian to visit the class and demonstrate proper pet care to the children.
- Read *Millions of Cats* by Wanda Gag (New York: Coward-McCann, 1938).

III-123   PARAKEET HOP

Subject Areas: Math and Movement

Concepts/Skills: Understands that each animal needs its own kind of food and shelter
Recognizes and places cardinal numbers in sequential order
Hops four times on each foot

Objective: The children will play a number game about a pet and its food.

Materials: • Orange paper carrot shape (see pattern) for each child
• Pet parakeet
• Markers
• Large open area
• Real carrot

Procedure:

1. Bring a pet parakeet to school in a cage and allow the children to observe it. Point out how the parakeet hops around the cage and makes noises. Place a real carrot in the cage and watch the parakeet peck away at it.

2. After observation and discussion of the parakeet's food, shelter, and movement, play "Parakeet Hop." Begin by numbering the paper carrots from 1 to 10. (Duplicate the numbers for a larger class.) Place the carrots in the center of a circle in which the children are standing. Have each child take a turn becoming a parakeet and hop on one foot to the center of the circle, pick up a carrot, and switch feet to hop back to the circle. (Make the distance from the circle to its center about four hops.) When the child gets back to the circle, ask him or her to name the numeral written on the carrot.

3. Continue until each child has had a turn picking up a carrot.

Variations/Ways to Extend:

• After this game is over, have the parakeets (children) hop into a line in which they place their numerals in proper sequential order from 1 to 10.
• Read *Fly High, Fly Low* by Don Freeman (New York: Viking Press, 1972).

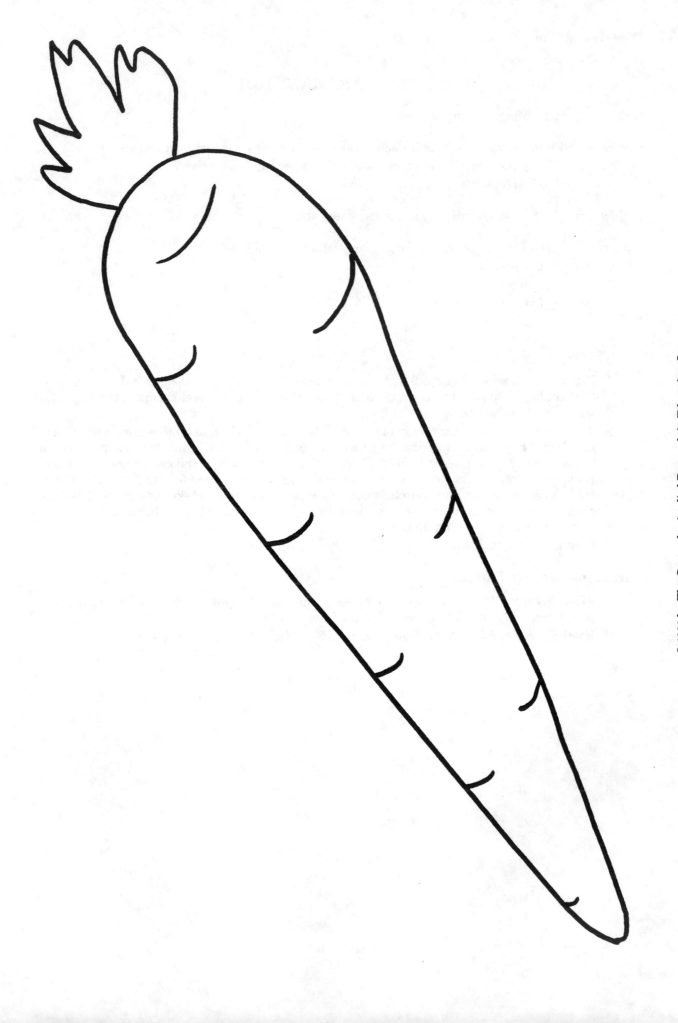

© 1986 by The Center for Applied Research in Education, Inc.

III–124   DOGGY, DOGGY, WHO HAS THE BONE?

Subject Area: Thinking Games

Concepts/Skills: Listens to directions for games and activities
Pays attention and concentrates on a task

Objective: The children will engage in a listening game about a common pet.

Materials:
- Large open area
- Object to represent food

Procedure:

1. Choose one child as the "Dog" to sit in the center of a circle of children with his or her head down and eyes closed. Place a "bone" (any object) behind the "Dog" and choose another child to sneak up to the "Dog," grab the "bone," go back to his or her position in the circle, and hide the "bone" behind him- or herself. Then have all the children put their hands behind themselves and say, "Doggy, doggy, who has the bone?" Tell the "Dog" to open his or her eyes and take three chances to guess who has the "bone."
2. Tell the children beforehand that the child with the "bone" may bark occasionally so that the "Dog" can try to determine where the bark came from.

Variation/Way to Extend:

- Use other common household pets with their food and sound to play this game, such as "Kitten, kitten, who has the milk?" and the child who has it purrs; or "Birdie, birdie, who has the birdseed?" and the child who has it chirps or whistles.

III-125 FISH AQUARIUM

Subject Area: Art

Concepts/Skills: Reproduces shapes (square and rectangle)
Uses scissors with control to cut on a line
Pays attention and concentrates on a task
Explores new materials

Objectives: The children create a picture of a fish tank by drawing, cutting, and pasting.

Materials: • Construction paper in various colors
• Crayons
• Scissors
• Paste
• Blue cellophane
• Tape or stapler

Procedure:

1. Using a model, show the children how to reproduce the shape of a square or a rectangle by drawing four attached lines. Have the children draw this on construction paper as the fish aquarium.
2. On a different color paper, have the children draw little fish to cut out. Paste these inside the lines of the fish tank. If they want, let the children add further details by coloring in snails, plants, gravel, and so on.
3. Give each child a sheet of blue cellophane to place over the picture to simulate water. Assist the child in stapling or taping this in place.

Variations/Ways to Extend:

• Read *Swimmy* by Leo Lionni (New York: Pantheon, 1963).
• Let the children choose their own ideas for a picture, such as a dog in a doghouse or a bird in a cage.

III-126   MY ZOO STORY

Subject Area: Social Studies

Concepts/Skills: Uses correct past, present, and future verb forms
Recognizes some words in own experience story

Objectives: The children will participate in a trip and/or discussion about the zoo and dictate an experience story about it.

Materials: • Excursion to a zoo or a visit from zoo personnel
• Chart paper
• Marker

Procedure:

1. Visit the zoo as a class or invite an animal caregiver for a visit. Talk about the many aspects of zoos—a place where we can safely see wild animals and where they are kept in cages or fenced in caves, fields, or water pools. Explain that animals often live longer in zoos than in their natural habitats because they are protected and receive good nourishment and health care.

2. Invite the children to ask questions of the zookeeper about his or her job and about their favorite zoo animals (questions about feeding, sounds, cleanliness, natural settings, and so on).

3. After the trip or visit is over, ask each child to dictate an experience story, and you write it out on chart paper. Encourage each child to look at the words carefully as you say and write them out. Most children will recognize at least a few of the words. Display the stories and refer to them often so that the children will recognize more words.

Variations/Ways to Extend:

• Read *Animals in the Zoo* by Feodor Rojankovsky (New York: Knopf, 1962).
• Encourage the children to make their favorite zoo animals from a mound of modeling clay.

III–127   ANIMAL HUNT

Subject Area: Creative Dramatics and Movement

Concepts/Skills: Takes initiative in learning
Proposes movement activity
Participates in imaginative play

Objective: The children will interpret the actions of their peers as they dramatize the actions of various animals.

Materials: • Large open area
• Chairs

Procedure:

1. Divide the class into two groups. Have one group sit in chairs lined up two-by-two to simulate a bus. Ask the other group to stand some distance away and wait for your instructions. With the latter group, whisper the name of an animal in the children's ears and ask this group to act out the animal's actions. For example, if you whisper "elephants," each child demonstrates the movement and sound of an elephant in his or her own way.

2. Ask the children on the bus to guess what animal is being represented. Do this for elephants, bears, giraffes, monkeys, lions, zebras, tigers, ostriches, seals, and other zoo animals. After several minutes, reverse the groups.

Variations/Ways to Extend:

• Play a thinking game called "Guess the Zoo Animal," for which the children take turns devising riddles for the others to solve. For example:

I have baggy skin. I am *very* big. I pick up peanuts with my long nose. *(elephant)*	I am small. I am funny. I like to copy. I have a long, curly tail. *(monkey)*
I am big. I have a loud roar. I am the king of the jungle. *(lion)*	I have feathers. I have a beak. I put my head into a hole in the ground. *(ostrich)*

• Read the Caldecott Medal book *The Biggest Bear* by Lynd Ward (Boston: Houghton-Mifflin, 1952). It is a story in which a boy captures a bear cub.

III-128 WATER, LAND, OR AIR?

Subject Area: Math

Concepts/Skills: Identifies a set as a collection of objects having a common property
Makes a simple comparison of objects (same/different)

Objectives: The children will classify animals according to their customary habitat and compare likenesses and differences.

Materials:
- Three sheets of 9″ × 12″ oaktag
- Three sheets of 9″ × 6″ oaktag
- Markers
- Pictures
- Cardboard
- Stapler
- Clear self-stick vinyl
- Glue

Procedure:

1. Staple the smaller sheets of oaktag onto the larger sheets so that three large pockets are formed. Label the backsheets "In the Water," "On the Land," and "In the Air," respectively, and let a child draw appropriate pictures for each on the pocket as shown in the accompanying illustration.

2. Supply many pictures of animals mounted on cardboard and covered with clear self-stick vinyl. Have the children work at the three pockets by classifying the animal pictures into the habitats in which the animals usually dwell.

3. You can do this activity individually or in small groups with the picture cards being placed into the correct pockets. You can also use the picture cards to compare animals. Ask, "In what ways are they the same?" "In what ways are they different?" "How are they like us?" "How are they different?"

Variations/Ways to Extend:

- Read *How, Hippo!* by Marcia Brown (New York: Scribner's, 1972).
- Read the poem "Furry Bear" by A. A. Milne, found in his book of poetry *Now We Are Six* (New York: Dell, 1975).

Weekly Subtheme: Zoo Animals

III-129 MONKEYS!

Subject Area: Language Arts

Concepts/Skills: Names words that rhyme

Supplies rhyming word to rhyme with a word given by the teacher

Objective: The children will listen to a fingerplay about an animal found in most zoos.

Materials:
- Words to the fingerplay
- Scissors
- Glue
- Paper
- Magazines

Procedure:

1. Teach the following fingerplay to the children, lowering each of five fingers as the words are said. Or, you might have five different children act out the verses.

Five Little Monkeys

Five little monkeys jumping on the bed,
One fell off and bumped his head,
Mommy called the doctor and the doctor said,
"That's what you get for jumping on the bed!"
Four little monkeys jumping . . .
Three little monkeys jumping . . .
Two little monkeys jumping . . .
One little monkey jumping on the bed,
He fell off and bumped his head,
Mommy called the doctor and the doctor said,
"That's what you get for jumping on the bed!"

2. After teaching the fingerplay and having the children enjoy the humor, use the fingerplay for pointing out rhyming words. Exaggerate the last word in every line and ask the children to tell you which words sound alike. Then have them generate a list of other words that rhyme with these, such as *fed, led, Ned, red,* and *Ted.*

3. Make little rhyme booklets by scouting through magazines together to find pictures of words that rhyme. Have the children cut these out and paste two or three pictures of words that rhyme on each page.

Variation/Way to Extend:

- Draw monkey heads and torsos with separate arms, legs, and tails and have the children cut them out on the lines. Punch holes in the torsos, limbs, and tails and have the children attach the parts with paper fasteners for movable monkeys.

III-130   ANIMAL MOSAICS

Subject Area: Art

Concept/Skill: Explores new materials

Objectives: The children will draw and fill in zoo animal pictures.

Materials:
- Lunch bags
- Rice
- Powdered tempera paints
- White posterboard squares
- Glue
- Containers
- Felt-tip markers
- Spoons

Procedure:

1. Let the children take turns pouring a small amount of rice into a lunch bag and adding powdered tempera in their choice of color. Have the children close the bag and shake it to coat and color the rice, and then pour the rice into a container. Repeat this procedure until the group has made several colors with which to work.
2. Next, have each child draw a zoo animal picture on a square of white posterboard. Let them squeeze or brush glue onto the areas of their pictures where they want color or texture. Then have the children spoon the colored rice onto those glued sections. Be sure to let the glue dry before shaking off the excess rice.

Variations/Ways to Extend:

- Let the children have a more free-form art experience by providing them with paper, felt-tip pens, crayons, and chalk to make any kind of zoo pictures they want.
- Read *The Animals Who Changed Their Colors* by Pascale Allamand, Elizabeth W. Taylor, tr. (New York: Lothrop, 1979).

III-131 SEE THE CIRCUS!

Subject Area: Social Studies

Concepts/Skills: Speaks in sentences
Makes relevant verbal contributions
Identifies expressions of feelings

Objectives: The children will participate in a conversation about and take an imaginary trip to the circus.

Materials:
- Books
- Records
- Pictures
- Popcorn

Procedure:

1. Begin a discussion with the children about the circus. Display pictures and books and listen to recordings about circuses.

2. If possible, visit a circus or have a member of a circus troupe visit the class. Explain that circus animals are animals that we talked about when discussing the farm, the forest, and the zoo and that these animals (usually elephants, bears, lions, tigers, and horses) are specially trained to perform.

3. Take an imaginary trip with the children to the circus and let them describe what they see. Pop some popcorn to eat and pretend that everyone is in the audience watching the acts. Ask, "Do you see the elephants touching trunk-to-tail and running around the arena or tent?" "How about the trapeze artists, lions, and tigers in the cage with their trainer?" "Do you see the clowns on stilts, tightrope walkers, and the bareback riders?" "Look at the ringmaster and the trainers on the elephants' backs!" "Smell the popcorn, peanuts, frankfurters, and cotton candy. What a wonderful place!" "How do the clowns feel?" "How do you know?"

Variations/Ways to Extend:

- Listen to the album *The Circus,* available from David C. Cook Publishing Company, 850 N. Grove Street, Elgin, IL 60120.

- For background music this week, play a recording of "Clowns" from *A Midsummer Night's Dream* by Mendelssohn.

III-132 CIRCUS DAY

Subject Area: Creative Dramatics and Movement

Concepts/Skills: Role plays
Places items in sequence
Cooperates in a group

Objective: The children will demonstrate through role playing what occurs at the circus.

Materials:
- Yarn
- Scissors
- Tape
- Makeup ingredients
- Circus props
- Clothes and hats

Procedure:

1. Discuss with the children the idea that at the circus the action often is going on simultaneously in the three big rings that form the show area of the tent or arena.

2. Simulate a three-ring circus by taping three large circles of heavy yarn to the floor. Encourage the children to assume some of the circus roles discussed this week. For those who wish to be clowns, use cold cream mixed with a little food coloring to apply facial features. Or use a watercolor brush and apply water-soluble acrylic paint to outline funny mouths, eyebrows, teardrops, flowers, or geometric shapes. Let the children don silly hats and frilly bibs from the dress-up area. Put a top hat on the ringmaster and give him or her a pretend microphone. Give a whip cut from yarn to the lion tamer and some small foam balls to the jugglers. In short, use whatever is available to re-create some of the excitement of the circus.

3. Let the children take turns role playing their acts in the three rings. As they become increasingly comfortable with the idea, let them try acting simultaneously as they do "under the big top."

Variation/Way to Extend:

- Invite parents to costume the children and have them be the audience for Circus Day.

III-133   LONG TRUNK/SHORT TRUNK

Subject Area: Math

Concept/Skill: Identifies size differences (big/little, long/short, large/small)

Objective: The children will use circus cut-outs to make determinations about size.

Materials: • Individual flannelboards
• Felt cut-outs of circus-animal shapes

Procedure:

1. Let the children use their individual flannelboards for this activity. Give them an assortment of *big* and *little* felt horses and ask them to sort these into two groups on the flannelboards. They can put a thin strip of felt down the center of the flannelboard to make separate areas.
2. Next, give them felt elephants, some with *long* trunks, others *short,* and let them sort these.
3. Then give them felt bear shapes, some *large* and some *small,* and likewise sort these into two groups.
4. Also using the horses and the bears, let each child demonstrate an understanding of which is bigger than the other and which is smaller than the other.

Variations/Ways to Extend:

• Read *The Mouse & the Elephant* by Joan Hewett (Boston: Little, Brown, 1977).
• Obtain an 11″ × 14″ art reproduction of "Bareback Riders" by W. H. Brown from the National Gallery of Art, Publications Service, Washington, DC 20565. Be sure to write for a catalog and prices.
• Encourage the children to move like horses (galloping, prancing, and so on). While doing this, play "Grand Canyon Suite" by Grofe, available from Bowmar Orchestral Library, Belwin Mills Publishing Corporation, 25 Deshon Drive, Melville, NY 11746.

III-134   PAINTED WAGONS

Subject Area: Language Arts

Concept/Skill: Verbalizes a fingerplay

Objective: The children will participate in a fingerplay about the circus.

Material: • Words to the fingerplay

Procedure:

1. Teach the following fingerplay to the children:

> Ten circus wagons, painted oh so gay, *(hold up ten fingers)*
> Rode into town with the circus today!
> In this one is a lion
> That gives a big loud roar! *(wiggle thumb on one hand)*
> In this one is a tiger
> Fast asleep upon the floor; *(wiggle index finger)*
> In this one is a funny seal
> That bows to left and right; *(wiggle middle finger)*
> In this one is a zebra
> With stripes all black and white; *(wiggle ring finger)*
> In this one is a camel
> With two lumps upon his back; *(wiggle little finger)*
> In this one is a panther
> That has shiny fur so black; *(wiggle thumb on other hand)*
> In this one is an elephant
> That is drinking from a pail; *(wiggle index finger)*
> In this one is a monkey
> That is hanging by his tail; *(wiggle middle finger)*
> In this one is a hippo
> With his smile so very wide; *(wiggle ring finger)*
> In this one is a leopard
> With a gaily spotted hide; *(wiggle little finger)*
> Ten circus wagons, painted oh so gay,
> Rode into town with the circus today! *(wiggle all ten fingers)*

2. Let the children repeat the fingerplay several times if they want.

Variation/Way to Extend

• Prepare felt animal shapes so that the children can use the flannelboard as the fingerplay is told. Or choose several animal shapes for the children to color. Then have them hold up the animals as each one is named during the fingerplay.

III-135   HAPPY CLOWN/SAD CLOWN

Subject Area: Art

Concepts/Skills: Identifies expressions of feelings
Reproduces basic shapes without a model

Objective: The children will create clown faces reflecting various emotions.

Materials: • Construction paper
• Glue
• Scissors
• Crayons
• Yarn
• Buttons

Procedure:

1. Start a discussion with the children about the way they feel when different things happen to them. Ask, "What makes you happy? Sad? Angry? Afraid? Surprised? Shy? Lonely? Disappointed?" and so on. Ask the children to show you how they look when they are feeling each of these emotions. Tell them to notice how others' eyes and mouths change to show the feelings talked about.

2. Explain that in the circus, clowns are made up to look happy, surprised, and so on. Talk about how circuses use tents to house the performances. Show the children how to draw a simple circus tent by drawing a square and then drawing a triangle on top. Add a scalloped line across for detail. Now ask the children to draw in the tent two large circles that will be clown heads. Give them buttons to glue on for eyes and have the children draw in noses. Now tell them to choose two feelings from the ones discussed and paste the yarn in such a way as to make mouths that turn up, turn down, or are in a circle (or some other position) to show the feelings.

3. To finish the clowns, have the children glue curly strands of yarn to the sides of the heads and add hats and bow ties.

Variation/Way to Extend:

• Read *Circus* by Beatrice S. De Regniers and Al Giese (New York: Viking Press, 1966).

SPRING

- ○ A New Beginning
- ○ Plant Life
- ○ Air, Rain, and Sunshine
- ○ The Balance of Nature

III–136   WHAT HAVE YOU DONE?

Subject Area: Creative Dramatics and Movement

Concepts/Skills: Controls body movement
Develops locomotor skills
Places items in sequence

Objective: The children will engage in creative movement to express their emotions or thoughts about some signs of spring.

Material: • Large open area

Procedure:

1. Precede the activity with some easy bending and stretching warmup exercises.
2. Then gather the children in a group, sit on the floor, and explain that you are going to mention various activities that some of them have probably done. Tell them that when they hear a familiar one that they would like to act out, they can say so or raise their hand, depending on your classroom's procedures. You might, for example, ask "Have you . . .

> . . . flown a kite?"
> . . . played hopscotch outside?"
> . . . watched birds drinking?"
> . . . caught frogs in a pond?"
> . . . been in a boat?"
> . . . splashed in a puddle?"
> . . . blown dandelion seeds?"
> . . . collected rocks?"
> . . . rolled in the grass?"
> . . . watched clouds in the sky?"
> . . . gone fishing and caught a fish?"
> . . . gone swimming?"
> . . . planted a garden?"
> . . . fed ducks?"
> . . . walked on the beach and collected shells?"

Variations/Ways to Extend:

- Instead of having the children act out what they have done, vary the items by instructing the children to "be the thing." For example, say, "Be the frogs in the pond." "Be the fish to be caught." "Be the duck to be fed."
- Read a verse from William Blake's poem "Spring."

SPRING

Little Lamb
Here I am;
Come and lick
My white neck;
Let me pull
Your soft wool;
Let me kiss
Your soft face;
Merrily, merrily, welcome in the Year.

III-137 THINK SPRING!

Subject Area: Social Studies

Concepts/Skills: Makes a simple comparison
Responds to nondirective questions
Proposes alternate ways of doing

Objectives: The children will participate in a discussion about spring and respond to some high-level questions.

Materials:
- Pictures of spring items
- List of questions
- Glue
- Oaktag
- Scissors

Procedure:

1. Begin a discussion about how people, animals, and plants come alive in the spring season. Cut out magazine pictures of eggs, chicks, bunnies, birds, and so on and mount each one on oaktag. Use these to stimulate the discussion and to ask high-level questions.

2. Begin with narrow questions that check the children's level of comprehension about spring and about the items pictured; then proceed to some broader questions that cause the children to analyze and synthesize their information. Here are some examples:

   How is a bunny different from a chick?

   Is spring colder or warmer than winter?

   What would you do if you were a bird and it began to rain outside?

   Would you like to live where it is sunny and warm all year long? Why? (Vary this question depending on your particular area.)

   What can you tell me about this picture?

   What is something else that is like a flower? A leaf? A cloud? An egg?

   How are plants and babies alike?

   What would you do if you were a flower and you grew upside down? What would you say?

Variations/Ways to Extend:

- Plan a field trip to a hatchery where the children can observe the egg-to-chick process first hand. Or, contact your farm extension representative and borrow an automatic-turning egg incubator for classroom use.
- Read *Horton Hatches the Egg* by Dr. Seuss (New York: Random House, 1954), which can be found in most libraries.

III-138 BALL IN THE FLOWERPOT

Subject Area: Gross Motor Games

Concepts/Skills: Throws a ball overhand and underhand
Throws a ball up in the air and catches by self

Objectives: The children will demonstrate throwing and catching skills in a game about spring.

Materials:
- Decorated wastebasket
- Three large rubber balls
- Masking tape
- Large open area

Procedure:

1. Before doing this activity, decorate a wastebasket with the children's pictures of flowers and plants.
2. Use the tape to designate a throwing line on the floor. Have each child take a turn stepping up to the line, opposite the "flowerpot" wastebasket that has been placed six feet away.
3. Give each child the three balls and tell him or her to try to throw the balls into the basket, one at a time. Demonstrate to the children how to throw overhand and underhand and have them practice throwing both ways into the basket. Talk about who got "one out of three" in or "two out of three" or "all of the balls" into the basket. Play this for a few rounds.

4. Next, have three children stand in an open area with plenty of space around each. Have each child take one of the balls, throw it up in the air, and try to catch it. Let the children have several tries; then have three other children take turns until everyone has had a chance.

Variation/Way to Extend:

- If a child is having difficulty with the skill of catching, you can roll a ball on the ground for him or her to catch. You can likewise help a child improve his or her throwing ability by taping a paper target on the ground or on a wall with which the child can practice.

III–139 SPRING BOARD!

Subject Area: Math

Concept/Skill: Places the cardinal numerals in sequential order from 0 to 10

Objectives: The children will make a collage background for a math readiness chart and use it to practice placing items in sequence.

Materials
- Oaktag
- Scissors
- Pictures of spring items
- Paste
- Marker
- Stapler

Procedure:

1. Position two sheets of oaktag vertically. From one sheet, cut a strip about two inches wide and staple it to the bottom of the other sheet so that a pocket is formed.

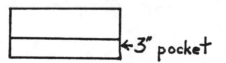

2. Have the children cut out spring pictures (nests with eggs, trees in bloom, flowers, umbrellas, bunnies, and so on) and paste them all over the back sheet.

3. Make cards of the cardinal numbers from 0 to 10 and let the children practice putting them in sequence by placing them across the pocket in proper order. Be sure that the cards are at least one inch longer than the height of the pocket and that the numbers are written in the upper portion so that they can be seen clearly.

Variation/Way to Extend:

- Use the pocket to introduce the numerals from 11 to 20 and show their proper sequence visually. Or make alphabet cards and let the children practice putting in sequence the letters of the alphabet, using four letters at a time, such as L/M/N/O.

Weekly Subtheme: A New Beginning

III-140 I SPY ...

Subject Area: Thinking Games

Concepts/Skills: Develops visual discrimination
Labels common items
Describes a simple object

Objectives: The children will play a game in which they find and describe pictures of spring items.

Materials: • Mounted pictures of spring items

Procedure:

1. To begin the game, hide five picture cards of spring items around the room, where they can be found by the children without too much difficulty. Have five children hide their eyes while you do this.
2. One at a time, ask the five children to look for the picture cards and to say "I spy a yellow flower" or whatever they have found. Ask each child to bring the found picture back to the group.
3. When all the pictures have been found, ask the first five children to hide them for another five children to find.

Variations/Ways to Extend:

• Use real objects instead of pictures to hide around the room.
• Listen to a cassette entitled "World of Nature" available from Belwin Mills Publ. Corp., Melville, N.Y. 11747.

Weekly Subtheme: Plant Life

III-141 THINK ABOUT SPRING!

Subject Area: Thinking Games

Concepts/Skills: Participates nonverbally in imaginative play
Identifies a set as a collection of objects having a common property
Works and plays cooperatively with others

Objectives: The children will identify signs of spring and play an imaginative game.

Material: • Pictures

Procedure:

1. Show the children pictures of various aspects of spring (plants, flowers in bloom, trees, grass, and so on).
2. Ask each child, one at a time, to think of one thing that reminds him or her of spring and to whisper that answer into your ear. You, in turn, whisper back to that child and suggest how to nonverbally act out (pantomime) the idea for the other children to guess. Some ideas are planting a seed or pretending to be a tree or a flower blooming.

Variations/Ways to Extend:

• Organize an art experience by having the children create a spring mural. Have the children paint some of the signs of spring on their mural. You might divide the long sheet of paper with light pencil lines so that each child has a specific area to fill. This minimizes "territorial" problems. Let the children then collect actual spring items during a spring walk and add these concrete objects to the mural.

• Play a recording of "Pretty Trees Around the World" by Ella Jenkins, from the album *Rhythms of Childhood* (Scholastic Records).

Weekly Subtheme: Plant Life

III-142 GARDEN DOMINOES

Subject Area: Language Arts

Concept/Skill: Distinguishes words that begin with the same sound

Objective: The children will identify letter sounds in the initial position by playing a domino game based on gardening items.

Materials:
- Colored index cards
- Pictures of gardening items
- Glue

Procedure:

1. Cut out pictures of items related to gardening and plant life (seeds, soil, pots, spades, shovels, plants, rain, sun, flowers, rake, bulbs, leaves, roots, light, and so on). Develop a set of domino cards by pasting two different pictures on an index card, each picture beginning with a different letter sound.

2. Ask the children to match like sounds by finding pictures on cards that begin with the same sound and placing them end to end as in dominoes.

Variation/Way to Extend:

- Use the picture cards to talk about other aspects of sound. You might ask, for example, "Do the items pictured make a sound when you tap them?" "Is it a loud or soft sound?" "High or low?" "Do they rustle in the wind or do they go pitter-patter?"

III-143 MAKE A FLOWER!

Subject Area: Art and Science

Concepts/Skills: Understands concepts of parts and the whole
Explores new materials
Develops fine motor movement

Objectives: The children will analyze the parts of real plants and construct their own versions of flowers and plants.

Materials:
- Collection of cut plants and flowers
- Magnifying glass
- Pipe cleaners
- Tissue paper
- Toothpicks
- Green florist tape
- Construction paper
- Small paper cups
- Cellophane tape

Procedure:

1. Take apart a wide variety of plants and flowers and let the children examine the parts with a magnifying glass. (You can collect plants and flowers on a walk or obtain fresh discards from your local florist.) Point out the flowers, leaves, stems, roots, and seeds where possible.
2. Set out the other materials listed and encourage the children to create their own flowers from what is available. Let the children combine what they learned from examining the plants with details from their own creative whimsy.

Variations/Ways to Extend:

- As a bulletin board, use yarn to have the children match the picture of a fruit with the picture of its product. Use actual labels from jars, cans, and cartons to enliven the chart further.

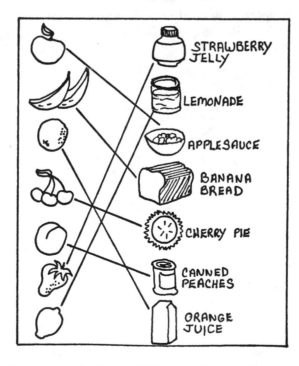

- Obtain an 11" x 14" art reproduction of "Vase of Chrysanthemums" by Claude Monet (No. 1845) from the National Gallery of Art, Publications Service, Washington, DC 20565. Be sure to write for a catalog and prices.

III-144   SEED SPECIMEN BOX

Subject Area: Science

Concepts/Skills: Records by exhibiting
Understands that many foods we eat come from seeds and plants

Objectives: The children will conclude that each type of fruit or flower has its own kind of seed and will learn how to construct a useful display box for collections.

Materials:
- Variety of seeds
- Pictures of mature plants produced by those seeds
- Shirt boxes
- Pencil
- Ruler
- Rolls of cotton
- Utility knife
- Scissors
- Glue
- Tape
- Plastic wrap

Procedure:

1. On a box cover, draw a ½-inch margin along all four sides. Cut the inside part out with a utility knife. Cut sheets of plastic wrap to fit inside the cover and tape them in place from the inside to create a window effect.
2. Let the children fill the box with cotton.
3. Arrange the seed samples as desired and place the pictures of the mature plants beneath each seed group to label. Glue in place. Replace the cover and let the children admire the collection through the "window."

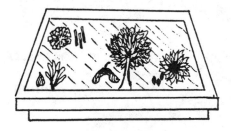

Variation/Way to Extend:

- Use the wonderful poem "Maytime Magic" by Mabel Watts to make a poetry poster for this activity.

III-145   SPONGE PLANTS TO GRAPH

Subject Area: Math

Concepts/Skills: Observes
Compares and places items of different sizes in order

Objectives: The children will identify types of seeds, make sponge plants, and graph the results of growth.

Materials:
- Quick-sprouting seeds (marigold, pumpkin, grass, mustard, parsley)
- Flat container
- Scissors
- Sponges
- Chart paper
- Marker

Procedure:

1. Cut sponges into various shapes reflecting the theme of spring (flowers, birds, clouds, bunnies, chicks, kites, and so on).

2. Let each child choose a sponge shape and a seed type. Have the children sprinkle the cut sponges with plenty of one variety of seed, place in a flat container, and keep moist.

3. Help the children graph the results of growth. Two kinds of graphs may be constructed from this activity:

Sprouting Graph

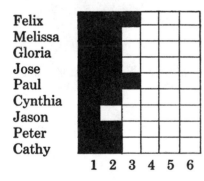

(Tape samples of the seed alongside each child's name to the left of the graph. Chart the number of days it took the seeds to sprout.)

Growth Graph

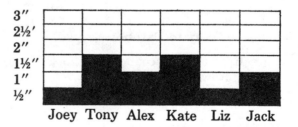

(Tape samples of the seed underneath each child's name at the bottom of the graph. Chart the growth in inches as the plants mature.)

Variations/Ways to Extend:

- Make sequence cards showing different stages in the development of one of the seeds mentioned here. Ask the children to arrange the cards to show the proper sequence of plant growth.
- Discuss possible reasons (amount of sunlight, water, dryness, or age of seed) for some seeds' sprouting more or less quickly than others.
- Do this activity with a variety of plant seeds and compare the growth of the different types.

III-146   THE POETRY OF RAIN

Subject Area: Language Arts

Concepts/Skills: Listens to poetry
Becomes aware of mood and use of words for imagery

Objective: The children will listen to a poem that creates a tranquil mood in describing rainfall and to another with a quicker rhythm.

Materials:
- Words to "April Rain Song"
- Words to "Rain"
- Marker
- Chart paper
- Paper raindrops or children's drawings

Procedure:

1. Read "April Rain Song" from *The Dream Keeper* by Langston Hughes (New York: Knopf, 1932). (**Note:** Although this book is out of print, a copy may be available in your library.) Talk with the children about the feelings of calmness it produces and then read it again for them. Print the words on a large sheet of chart paper and use it as a focal point for a wall display or bulletin board about rain. Add raindrops cut from paper or children's drawings of rain to create a scene.

2. Compare the reading of "April Rain Song" to that of "Rain" by Robert Louis Stevenson, which has a quicker rhythm.

RAIN
The rain is falling all around,
It falls on field and tree,
It rains on the umbrellas here,
And on the ships at sea.

Variation/Way to Extend:

- Read the Caldecott Honor book *The Storm Book* by Charlotte Zolotow (New York: Harper & Row, 1952).

III-147 BUBBLE PAINT

Subject Area: Art

Concepts/Skills: Explores new materials
Expresses self creatively

Objectives: The children will observe how air being whipped into a liquid medium can change its consistency, and they will paint with the tinted substance.

Materials:
- ½ cup soapflakes for each child
- 2 tablespoons liquid starch for each child
- Paper
- Electric mixer or eggbeater
- Food coloring
- Containers
- Brushes
- Bowls

Procedure:

1. Demonstrate how whipping air bubbles into a starch-and-soapflakes mixture changes its consistency to one of thick, stiff bubbles. Let each child do this with the soapflakes and liquid starch.
2. Let each child choose a food color and tint the bowl of bubble mixture to make a paint substance. Let the children trade colors if desired.
3. Using the brushes, have the children create paintings of their own design. Let the paintings dry overnight and then display them at the children's eye-level.

Variation/Way to Extend:

- During dramatic play, supply a prop box of service station equipment. Introduce the tools, an inner tube, and an air pump.

III-148   RAINY-DAY FUN

Subject Areas: Language Arts and Creative Dramatics

Concepts/Skills: Acts out a story as teacher recites
Places items in sequence
Interprets the main idea of a story

Objective: The children will demonstrate the events in a story about rain.

Materials:
- Book or recording
- Outdoor hose and sprinkler
- Rainwear
- Umbrellas
- Large open area outdoors

Procedure:

1. After the children listen to a recording or reading of *Umbrella* by Taro Yashima (New York: Penguin, 1977), prepare them to act out the sequences of events presented in the story.
2. Play the role of the mother in the story who admonishes her child to wait for a rainy day to make use of the girl's much-treasured new umbrella. Have the children continue to plead for a chance to use their umbrellas until one day when the mother agrees that since it is raining, they can finally go out with their new umbrellas.
3. Arrange to have rubbers, raincoats, and umbrellas available for each child. Also arrange for a hose and sprinkler system to be turned on outdoors so that the children can enjoy their own rainy day.
4. Follow this activity with a discussion and ask, "What happens when it rains?" "What happens before it rains?" "Does it rain when it is sunny?" "Is rain hot?" "Find out if it is hot or cold." "How can we stay dry on a rainy day?"

Variation/Way to Extend:

- Make an audio book with the class. Let the children draw and color their impressions of rain falling in a pond, on a roof, with thunder, and so on. Make an audio tape of these scenes and use the tape as a stimulus for the drawings.

III-149 SUN TOWERS

Subject Area: Math

Concepts/Skills: Identifies sets of 0 to 5 members and constructs corresponding sets
Identifies an empty set as having no members
Solves simple verbal problems using numerals

Objective: The children will demonstrate building corresponding sets between numbers of suns and blocks

Materials:
- Two sets of cards with up to five suns on each one
- Container of small blocks

Procedure:

1. Place the cards face down. Have a child choose a card. Ask the child to count the number of suns on the card and say the number aloud. Then have the child take the corresponding number of blocks and build a tower.

2. Have the next child choose a card and do the same until all the children have had a turn.
3. Compare the towers by counting the blocks and by measuring. Ask, "If you have two blocks and I give you one more, how many will you have?" Explain that when all of the blocks are away, the table is empty. It has no blocks.

Variations/Ways to Extend:

- Read the poem "The Sun Travels" by Robert Louis Stevenson.
- Use the blocks to help the children add and subtract. Put down two blocks, count them with the children, and let the children touch them. Then put down another block and say, "Two blocks and one block are three blocks." "Three blocks and one are four." Four and one are five." "Five take away one is four," and so on.

Weekly Subtheme: Air, Rain, and Sunshine

III-150 BALLOON BOAT

Subject Area: Science

Concept/Skill: Observes the effect of air as wind

Objective: The children will generalize that air has force as they observe a balloon being released.

Materials:
- Quart-size milk cartons
- Stapler
- Tub of water
- Utility knife
- Long, thin balloons

Procedure:

1. Staple the spout of a milk carton together so that it is tightly sealed. Hold it horizontally and carefully cut out one side panel to make a hollow boat.

2. Now inflate a balloon and, holding the opening tightly, place the balloon in the carton and then the carton in the water. Release the balloon. Have the children watch the air in the balloon be released and push the boat around the water.

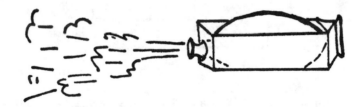

3. Make several of these balloon boats and let the children experiment with them or have races. Point out that the movement is opposite the direction of the released air.

Variations/Ways to Extend:

- To observe the effect of air on growth, compare the life of a plant in a jar with a lid with one in a jar without a lid. Guide the children in realizing that plants need air to stay alive and grow.
- Read the poem "Who Has Seen the Wind?" by Christina Rossetti.

WHO HAS SEEN THE WIND

Who has seen the wind?
 Neither I nor you:
But when the leaves hang trembling
 The wind is passing through.

Who has seen the wind?
 Neither you nor I:
But when the trees bow down their heads
 The wind is passing by.

Weekly Subtheme: Balance of Nature

III-151 ANIMAL TRACKS

Subject Area: Language Arts

Concepts/Skills: Shows understanding of present tense by properly using the verb form
Understands that animal life and other aspects of the environment should be respected

Objectives: The children will associate the tracks of animals with their names and describe their movements in the present tense.

Materials:
- Book
- Oaktag
- Construction paper
- Marker
- Scissors
- Pieces of cloth
- Tape

Procedure:

1. Select and draw the tracks of three animals on construction paper and cut them out. Sample tracks of a squirrel, raccoon, and deer, respectively, are shown here. Place the tracks on the floor. Be sure that each set of tracks leads to a wall where large pieces of oaktag are covered by pieces of cloth so that the children cannot see what is drawn on them.

2. Show the children the pictures in the book *Animal Tracks* by George F. Mason (New York: Morrow, 1943). (**Note:** Although this book is out of print, a copy may be in your library.).
3. Tell the children to follow each of the animal tracks to the wall, where the piece of oaktag is then uncovered. The oaktag following the deer tracks, for example, will contain a picture of a buck (male) or doe (female). Each picture contains a description of the animal's movement, written in the present tense. For example, this one might say, "The deer walks, trots, and leaps." Read the sentence to the children and have them move like a herd of deer (walking, trotting, and leaping).
4. Continue following the tracks to a picture of a raccoon. The sentences will read: "The raccoon climbs, walks, and runs." Allow the children to repeat the sentence and then move like raccoons. Continue following the tracks to a picture of a squirrel. The sentence reads: "The squirrel scampers, climbs, and leaps." Again, have the children repeat the sentence and move like squirrels.

Variation/Way to Extend:

- Read the Caldecott Honor book *Thy Friend, Obadiah* by Brinton Turkle (New York: Viking, 1969). It is a story about a boy and a seagull.

III-152   FEED THE BIRDS

Subject Area: Science

Concepts/Skills: Understands balance of nature
Develops fine motor movement
Understands that each animal needs its own kind of food

Objectives: The children will construct bird feeders, recall that birds eat seeds from plants, and conclude why it is important to provide seeds for birds.

Materials:
- Wild birdseed and/or suet
- Plastic half-gallon or gallon milk containers
- Pine cones
- Utility knife
- Peanut butter
- Ten-inch dowel (optional)
- String

Procedure:

1. Wash and thoroughly rinse the milk container. Cut out an opening, leaving a three-inch bottom to hold the seeds. Insert a ten-inch dowel across the opening as a perch if desired. Fill the bottom with seed or suet and hang from an easy-to-reach branch outdoors.

2. To make another type of birdfeeder, collect pine cones and allow the children to stuff each one with peanut butter before sprinkling with seeds. Using string, attach the pine cones to nearby tree branches.

3. Encourage the children to observe the birds eating the seed. Point out the fact that they are eating seeds that come from sunflower plants. Mention other animals, such as rabbits and snails, that rely on plants for food. Ask, "What plants do we eat in order to live?" "What seeds do we eat?" "Is it easier for birds to find seeds in warmer or cooler weather?" "It is a good idea to leave seeds for birds, especially when they may not be able to find many seeds. Why is it important to continue leaving seeds once birds begin to eat them?"

Variations/Ways to Extend:

- After observing the birds eating the seeds, have the children dictate a group story about the experience.
- Play a recording of "Wake Up Little Sparrow" by Ella Jenkins from the album *Rhythms of Childhood* (Scholastic).
- Read the Caldecott Medal book *A Tree Is Nice* by Janice M. Udry (New York: Harper & Row, 1956).

Weekly Subtheme: Balance of Nature

III–153   TREE OF LIFE

Subject Area: Art

Concepts/Skills: Explores new materials
Uses mixed media

Objectives: The children will paint, cut, paste, and print to create a tree design.

Materials:
- Color reproduction of Matisse's "Tree of Life"
- White paper
- Green paper
- Blue paint
- Yellow paint
- Glue
- Sponges
- Scissors
- Containers
- Brushes

Procedure:

1. Show the children the color reproduction of Henry Matisse's "Tree of Life" painting. **(Note: a 40″ × 18″ poster of "Tree of Life," No. B1964V, is available for a charge from the Metropolitan Museum of Art, 66-26 Metropolitan Avenue, Middle Village, NY 11379. A catalog of other reproductions is also available for a small fee.)** Let the children notice the way the artist made use of color, shape, and space.
2. Distribute the white paper and ask the children to paint these sheets blue. Allow a variety of effects to emerge.
3. While these sheets are drying, have the children cut leaf shapes from the green paper and glue them onto the blue-painted paper.
4. Distribute sponges that have been cut in a larger, wider, more organic leaf shape than the green paper leaves. Have the children dip these sponges into the yellow paint and print where they like on their papers.

Variation/Way to Extend:

- Use other artists' paintings to stimulate the children to achieve a variety of results when they work with art materials. For a Tiffany stained-glass look, for example, have the children draw a design with black felt-tip pens, then color in the sections with colored pencils or markers.

III-154   A HOUSE FOR A BLUEBIRD

Subject Area: Science

Concepts/Skills: Follows a series of dot-to-dot numerals from 1 to 10 to form an object
Uses scissors with control

Objectives: The children will gain appreciation for a beautiful bird and understand some of the problems associated with conservation.

Materials:
- Book
- Photographs
- Dot-to-dot illustration
- Scissors
- Blue markers or crayons

Procedure:

1. Introduce the children to the cheerful bluebird. Written for older children, the book *Bluebird Rescue* by Joan R. Heilman (New York: Lothrop, Lee and Shephard, 1982) might be helpful if you read parts of it, or interpret it for the children and show pictures of bluebirds.
2. Explain that these little songbirds are suffering a severe decline in population mainly because they are cavity-nesting birds (need an enclosure), and appropriate sites and habitats are becoming scarce for them. (**Note:** A woodworking project that can be partially accomplished by the children and has the potential to help the bluebird is mentioned under "Variation/Way to Extend.")
3. Distribute copies of the dot-to-dot illustration and tell the children to follow the numerals from 1 to 10. Let them color their birds blue and then cut them out. Display the bluebirds around the room.

Variation/Way to Extend:

- Write to the North American Bluebird Society, Box 6295, Silver Springs, MD 20906 for pictures, pamphlets, bluebird art prints, and plans for a simple nesting box design. Once the wood is cut to the proper dimensions, it is a simple project for the children to help complete by hammering in place.

© 1986 by The Center for Applied Research in Education, Inc.

III-155 NATURE MOBILE

Subject Area: Social Studies

Concepts/Skills: Develops fine motor movement
Explores new materials
Understands balance of nature

Objective: The children will construct mobiles to illustrate the idea of the balance of nature.

Materials:
- Straws
- String
- Pictures of nature items
- Stapler
- Oaktag
- Paste

Procedure:

1. Have the children collect pictures of nature items (trees, flowers, rocks, water scenes, the sun, animals, insects, and so on) by looking through magazines, catalogs, and brochures. Have them cut out the pictures and paste them onto oaktag.
2. Explain to the children what a mobile is and how it balances. Then show the children how to construct a simple mobile by cutting various lengths of string and tying them onto straws so that each straw hangs in balance with the others.
3. Staple the nature pictures to the ends of these strings. Talk about the interdependence of living things, using examples the children will understand—such as trees for habitats, shade, food, animals for food, and clothing.

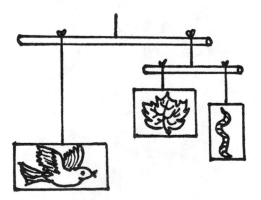

Variations/Ways to Extend:
- Do this activity with objects found on a nature walk, using real items rather than pictures.
- Read the Caldecott Medal book *Make Way for Ducklings* by Robert McCloskey (New York: Viking, 1941).

COMMUNITY WORKERS

○ Health Professionals—

Doctors, Nurses, Dentists

○ Police Officers and Firefighters

○ Shopkeepers and Office Workers

○ Librarians and Postal Workers

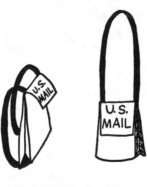

Weekly Subtheme: Health Professionals (Doctors, Nurses, Dentists)

III-156 OUR HOSPITAL CORNER

Subject Area: Creative Dramatics and Movement

Concepts/Skills: Acts out a story the teacher recites
Places items in sequence

Objectives: The children will realize the importance of doctors and act out the story *Madeline*.

Materials:
- Book
- Stuffed toy mouse
- Stuffed toy tiger
- Doctor's tools
- Cardboard box

Procedure:

1. Ask the children if they have ever been to a hospital. Engage them in a short discussion of their experiences.

2. Tell the children they are going to listen to a story about a little girl who had to go to the hospital. Read the Caldecott Honor book *Madeline* by Ludwig Bemelmans (New York: Penguin, 1977). After reading the story, ask, "Who made Madeline all better?" Stress the importance of doctors and the fact that they can be men or women.

3. Let the children act out the story, using the following scenes:

    All the children walk in straight lines, see a mouse, and get scared—except Madeline.

    The teacher uses a stuffed tiger, the children get scared, but Madeline says, "Pooh pooh."

    The children are asleep, but Madeline cries.

    Miss Clavel calls the doctor (a child) and rushes Madeline to a hospital (use a cardboard box as an ambulance).

    The doctor uses a stethoscope and other tools and pronounces Madeline healed.

    The children come to visit Madeline and play with her toys.

    The children pretend they are eating, brushing their teeth, and going to bed.

    When Miss Clavel comes in, they all say in unison, "Boo hoo, we want to have our appendix out, too!"

4. The children may want to play the "Madeline" game again later in the week. If so, see how well they can recall the sequence of the story themselves. (You may interject scenes when necessary.)

Variation/Way to Extend:

- Obtain one or more of the four "Madeline" stories available as read-along cassette and book sets from Kimbo Educational, P.O. Box 477A, Long Branch, NJ 07740.

III-157 MEDICAL RIDDLES

Subject Area: Thinking Games

Concept/Skill: Understands relationships

Objectives: The children will understand the importance of the doctor and answer riddles about what the doctor does.

Materials:
- Book about visiting the doctor
- Riddles

Procedure:

1. Read a book about visiting the doctor and ask specific riddles about the content.
2. Make up some riddles of your own, too. Here are some examples:

I am a person
who helps you get better
when you are sick.
I am a _____. (doctor, nurse)

I am a doctor's tool.
I help the doctor
listen to your heart.
I am a _____. (stethoscope)

I am a small light.
I help the doctor look
Into your throat.
I am a _____. (flashlight)

I am a wooden tool.
I push down on your
tongue.
I am a _____. (tongue depressor)

Variations/Ways to Extend:

- Ask the children the names of their pediatricians or family doctors. Ask the children's parents to take photos of them visiting their doctors. Display these photos with the children's and doctors' names labeled.
- Send for a small booklet entitled *First Aid for Little People* to Johnson & Johnson, Consumer Services Dept., New Brunswick, NJ 08903.

III–158 WHAT A DENTIST DOES

Subject Area: Science

Concepts/Skills: Listens to stories
Recalls information

Objectives: The children will discover the role of the dentist and the importance of proper tooth care.

Material: • Book

Procedure:

1. Take about ten minutes to read *My Friend, the Dentist* by Jane Werner Watson et al. (Racine, WI: Western, 1972) the first time and observe if the children can listen throughout. Have a discussion about visiting the dentist. Ask the children to describe their visits to the dentist. Discuss becoming a dentist as a career option for boys and girls when they grow to adulthood. Talk about brushing and flossing teeth correctly and about the proper foods for developing healthy teeth.

2. After a few minutes of physical exertion, go through the book a second time and see if the children can recall the information that was given on each page as they view the pictures.

Variation/Way to Extend:

• Make a prop box with dental equipment in it and have the children engage in dramatic play with dolls and the equipment. Include such items as toothbrushes, dental floss, small mirrors, plastic tools, cotton balls, small paper cups, a tray, and old photo negatives to use as X-ray film. Contact some dentists to see if they will contribute flat-ended dental tools that will otherwise be discarded because they have become dull. Let some children pretend to be dental assistants as well.

Weekly Subtheme: Health Professionals (Doctors, Nurses, Dentists)

III–159 STICK SETS

Subject Area: Math

Concept/Skill: Solves simple verbal problems using numerals

Objective: The children will add non-equivalent sets of tongue depressors.

Material: • Tongue depressors

Procedure:

1. Place ten tongue depressors on the table and have the children count them. Take two away from the pile and ask the children to count them. Take two more away from the pile and have the children count these. Put the two "new" sets side by side and show that two sticks and two sticks makes four sticks. Then do this with three sticks and two sticks. Repeat with one stick and four sticks.
2. Let the children continue to group and add the ten sticks.

Variations/Ways to Extend:

- Read *What Do You Want to Be?* by Françoise (New York: Scribner's, 1957).
- Record a pretend story about a day in the life of a doctor, nurse, ambulance driver, and so on.

III-160   LET'S BE NURSES

Subject Area: Social Studies

Concepts/Skills: Works and plays cooperatively
Tells function of body parts
Shows empathy toward other children

Objectives: The children will play with nurses' kits and make nurses' hats and arm bands.

Materials:
- Chairs
- Dolls
- Cotton
- Medicine bottles
- Plastic bottles
- Stapler
- Hats
- Tape measure
- Telephone
- Pads and pencils
- Tape
- Scissors
- Bags
- Bandages
- Stethoscope
- Syringes without needles
- White paper
- Marker
- Bobby pins

Procedure:

1. If possible, have the school nurse or a visiting nurse come and describe the job that a nurse does. Remind the children that boys as well as girls can grow up to be nurses.

2. Give each child a bag and some of the supplies listed above so that each has a nurse's kit. Have the children make nurses' hats by folding, cutting, and stapling white paper into the shape shown here and writing a name on it in red. These can be worn with bobby pins. You might also have the children make simple arm bands with the child's name and a red cross written on in red.

3. Talk about the various parts of the body with the children and explain how they are important. Pretend that someone is hurt and needs help. Ask, "How would you respond?"

Variations/Ways to Extend:

- Let the children listen to their heartbeats with a real stethoscope. Suggest that they exercise and then listen to the increased rate.
- Write to Coronet Films, 65 E. South Water Street, Chicago, Ill. 60601 for a catalog of the many films they have pertaining to the health and growth of the human body.

III-161 THE POLICE OFFICER AND THE LOST CHILD

Subject Area: Thinking Games

Concepts/Skills: Listens to directions for games
Refines logical thinking when dealing with relationships

Objective: The children will participate in a guessing game involving police officers.

Materials: • Several props
• Large open area

Procedure:

1. Use a police officer's hat and/or badge to designate one child (girl or boy) as the police officer. Have the rest of the group sit in a circle.
2. Pretend to be the parent of a lost child. Describe to the officer what the child (one of the children in the circle) looks like and is wearing. From the description, the police officer must identify the child and bring him or her to you. Then the "found" child becomes the police officer, and the game continues. Assist the children in keeping the descriptions simple.

Variations/Ways to Extend:

• Read *Policeman Small* by Lois Lenski (New York: Walck, 1962). (**Note:** Although this book is out of print, a copy may be available in your library.)
• Remind the children that both boys and girls can grow up to be police officers.

III–162   VISIT TO THE POLICE STATION

Subject Area: Social Studies

Concepts/Skills: Predicts realistic outcomes of events
Observes and compares

Objectives: The children will predict what they will see at a police station and then visit one.

Materials: • Arranged visit
• Transportation
• Fingerprinting equipment (optional)

Procedure:

1. Discuss with the children the job of being a police officer. Tell the children that officers enforce the rules that exist for everyone's safety. They also help people, including children, solve many day-to-day problems. Explain that a special school exists to train police officers to do their job.
2. Make arrangements to visit the local police station and prepare the children for the visit. Discuss what they expect to see there and then compare that list with what is actually found. With their parents' permission, the children might enjoy having their fingerprints taken there or back at school.

Variation/Way to Extend:

• When you return to the classroom, have the children draw pictures of what they observed at the police station. Label each child's picture.

III–163 FIVE POLICE OFFICERS

Subject Area: Language Arts

Concepts/Skills: Verbalizes a fingerplay
Places cardinal numerals in sequential order

Objective: The children will demonstrate a fingerplay about police officers.

Material: • Words to the fingerplay

Procedure:

1. Teach the following fingerplay to the children:

   Five police officers, standing by a store, (*hold up 5 fingers*)
   One directed traffic and then there were four. (*bend thumb down*)
   Four police officers watching over me,
   One took home a lost girl and then there were three. (*bend index finger*)
   Three police officers dressed all in blue,
   One stopped a speeding car and then there were two. (*bend middle finger*)
   Two police officers, how fast they can run,
   One caught a bank robber and then there was one. (*bend ring finger*)
   One police officer, standing in the sun,
   Sun went down, he went home, and then there were none. (*make fist*)

2. Let the children repeat the fingerplay several times if they like. Vary the pronoun in the last line so that the children are reminded that women can also be police officers.

Variation/Way to Extend:

• Dress five children in police officer garb (or give them each a paper badge to wear) to line up next to one another and act out the fingerplay. Have the children sit down, one at a time, first through fifth.

III-164   WE ARE FIREFIGHTERS!

Subject Area: Creative Dramatics and Movement

Concepts/Skills: Places items in sequence
Plays cooperatively
Acts out a story
Participates verbally and nonverbally in imaginative play

Objective: The children will dramatize a story about firefighting.

Materials: • Large open area
• Props (telephone, bell, old raincoats, boots, firefighter hats, pieces of hose, coffee cans, wagons, play tools, indoor climbing gym, and so on)

Procedure:

1. Encourage the children to choose some props and play firefighters on their own for a short time. Then tell them to listen to the story you are going to tell and to act out what they hear.
2. First, pretend to smell smoke. Say that you must call the fire department on the telephone. One of the firefighters (children) answers the call and sounds the alarm (rings a bell). The other firefighters gather and pretend to slide down a pole. Next, they put on their outfits— boots, raincoats, and hats. One firefighter drives the engine out, and all the other firefighters jump on. They pretend to be going very fast and make the sound of a siren. Soon they arrive at a burning building. They stop the engine and jump off. They use their hoses to put out the fire. Some of the firefighters put on oxygen tanks, pick up tools, and climb up the ladder to go into the building and check for people and pets. They find a puppy and carefully carry it down the ladder. All the people in the building have gotten out safely. The fire is out, and it is time for the firefighters to jump back on the engine and go back to the firehouse.

Variation/Way to Extend:

• Contact a local forest service of the U.S. Department of Agriculture for fire prevention materials, including posters and songs about Smokey the Bear.

III–165 FIRE AND SMOKE!

Subject Area: Language Arts

Concepts/Skills: Develops plot and sequence
Orally expresses self
Completes a statement of parallel relationships

Objectives: The children will participate in a discussion about firefighting and fill in the missing word of an unfinished statement.

Materials: • Pictures
• List of parallel statements

Procedure:

1. Talk with the children about the occupation of firefighting. Recall the dramatic play experiences given in Activity III–164.

2. Show the pictures of firefighters, equipment, and so on and explain that special schooling and training is needed to learn how to fight fires and handle equipment. Talk about fire engines, hook and ladder trucks, water pumpers, and neighborhood fire hydrants. Explain that firefighters are men and women who work to keep us safe. Ask the children to make up a story suggested by what they see in the pictures.

3. Have a list of parallel statements ready to read to the children and obtain their responses. Some examples are:

> Sand is dry. Water is ——— . (wet)
> Firefighters ride on an engine. They climb a ——— . (ladder)
> Ice is cold. Fire is ——— . (hot)
> We see with our eyes. We hear the alarm with our ——— . (ears)
> We can walk up steps. We can slide down a ——— . (pole)
> The telephone rings quietly. The siren is ——— . (loud)
> We see fire. We smell ——— . (smoke)

Variation/Way to Extend:

• Visit the local fire station or invite a firefighter to demonstrate some tools or equipment.

III-166   WHAT JOB IS THIS?

Subject Areas: Social Studies and Thinking Games

Concepts/Skills: Uses attributes of composition and use to describe
Predicts realistic outcome

Objective: The children will play a game in which they will examine various occupations.

Materials: • Objects from home
• Large open area

Procedure:

1. Send a note home asking parents to allow their child to bring something to school that reflects the occupation of one of the parents. Ask the parents to wrap the object or put it in a bag and label the wrapping with the child's last name.
2. Have the children sit in a circle, holding their concealed objects. Ask each child to take a turn describing the object and how it is used. Have the other children guess what the item is and what the occupation is. Then have the child unwrap the object and let everyone examine it.

Variation/Way to Extend:

• Take some instant photos of shops and other places of interest in the community. Use the photos as a source of discussion and display them in the room.

III–167 ELECTRICIAN'S ART

Subject Area: Art

Concepts/Skills: Develops creativity
Explores new materials
Understands form in space

Objective: The children will make a sculpture from wire.

Materials:
- Plastic-coated electrician's wire or 18-gauge wire, copper wire, colored telephone wire, or floral wire (one piece for each child)
- Staple gun
- Hammer
- Scrap pieces of sanded wood

Procedure:

1. Encourage each child to manipulate a small piece of wire about fifteen inches in length. Ask the children to make a design, an animal, or anything else they like with the wire. Give additional pieces of wire if desired.
2. Assist the children in attaching the finished sculpture to the wood block for stapling.

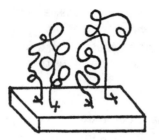

3. Allow each child to tell about his or her sculpture.

Variation/Way to Extend:

- Ask the children to name all the electrical appliances they can see in the room or that they have in their homes.

III-168   WHAT SHALL WE BE?

Subject Area: Creative Dramatics and Movement

Concepts/Skills: Understands concept of occupations
Role plays

Objective: The children will role play the occupations suggested by prop boxes.

Materials:
- Prop box for beautician (mirror, curlers, hairpins, hairnets, dryer, aprons, combs, towels, magazines, plastic bottles, basin, emery boards, pencil, paper, telephone, play money, and so on)
- Prop box for forest ranger (canteen, flashlight, rope, canvas for tent, mosquito netting, knapsack, food supplies, mess kits, nature books, small logs, a grill, binoculars, compass, and so on)
- Prop box for baker (hat, Play-Doh, bowls, cookie cutters, rolling pins, cookie sheets, cake pans, muffin tins, cupcake liners, sprinkles, a timer, wooden spoons, and so on)
- Prop box for office worker (pads, pens, pencils, carbon paper, paper clips, glue, an old typewriter, telephone, erasers, file folders, envelopes, rubber stamps and ink pads, and so on)

Procedure:

1. Prepare the proper boxes and let the children examine and discuss the contents. Encourage the boys and girls to examine each occupation.
2. Designate areas in the room for a beauty shop, a forest or camp site, a bakery, and an office and allow the children ample play time to let their imaginations soar.

Variation/Way to Extend:

- Ask the children to generate a list of items for use in prop boxes depicting other occupations. Collect them and follow the foregoing procedure.

III–169 MATH MACHINE

Subject Area: Math

Concepts/Skills: Recognizes numerals
Understands one-to-one correspondence
Forms a new set by joining two sets

Objective: The children will apply math skills by playing a game with a "machine."

Materials:
- Large box with one side cut off
- Small paper bags
- Bell
- Tape
- Prepared index cards
- Stool
- Paint or decorative self-stick vinyl
- Brushes (optional)
- Scissors (optional)
- Utility knife

Procedure:

1. Obtain a box large enough for a child to sit behind. Let the children either paint it or cover it with self-stick vinyl. Make several horizontal slits across the front of the box. Tape a paper bag on the inside of the box under each slit so that it will catch index cards pushed through.

2. Have the child behind the box look at each card as it comes through and solve the problem by demonstrating the answer with the bell. For example, start with cards showing numerals. If the child gets a card with a "3" on it, he or she rings the bell three times. If the child receives a card with four stickers on it, he or she rings the bell four times. If the child receives two cards, one with two flower stickers and another with three flower stickers, he or she rings the bell five times to show the joining of two sets.

Variation/Way to Extend:

- Use the machine for other math readiness activities. It lends itself well to sorting activities if labels, such as colors, shapes, animal categories, and so on, are pasted on the outside of the box under each slit. The machine could also be used for language arts to sort letters or sounds.

III-170   WHAT SHOULD I BUY?

Subject Areas: Language Arts and Thinking Games

Concept/Skill: Distinguishes words that begin with the same sound

Objective: The children will play a game in which they associate word and letter sounds.

Material: • Department store catalogs

Procedure:

1. Talk about the many items that can be found in a department store, a place with which most children will be familiar. Allow the children time to browse through the catalogs.
2. Invite the children to sit in a circle and think about the letter sounds in the words of the catalog items that interest them. Then say, "Who wants to buy something that begins with the sound of A?" After a few responses, move on to B, C, and so on through some of the alphabet. The children should respond with words that correspond to the letter being discussed.

Variation/Way to Extend:

• Make arrangements with a local store, such as a pet shop or hardware store, for the children to visit. Instruct the children to take note of how items are categorized, arranged, and so on.

III-171   LET'S PLAY LIBRARY

Subject Area: Creative Dramatics and Movement

Concepts/Skills: Works and plays cooperatively
Participates verbally in imaginative play

Objectives: The children will describe what they know about the library and through role playing demonstrate these ideas.

Material: • Library area in classroom

Procedure:

1. Set up an area in the room to be designated the "library." Provide a rug, tables, chairs, books, telephones, shoe boxes with colored index cards, book racks, ink pads, rubber stamps, and pretend library cards (file cards with a child's name on each).
2. Discuss the procedures at the library, how books are grouped, librarians' duties, and so on. Let the children tell what they know of other activities (films, story times, audio-visual machines, and so on) that take place at their local public libraries.
3. Allow the children to role play checking out books, stocking shelves, helping people find books, and so on.

Variation/Way to Extend:

• Declare a "Book Day" and have children bring in their favorite books from home or the library. Be sure that all are labeled with the children's names for identification. Display the books and read all of them over the course of several days.

III–172 MAKING CHOICES

Subject Area: Social Studies

Concepts/Skills: Responds to nondirective questions
Makes relevant verbal contribution

Objectives: The children will participate in a discussion about letter carriers and "vote" their opinions about certain statements.

Materials: • Pictures of the post office
• Pictures of letter carriers

Procedure:

1. Discuss with the children the jobs of postal workers and letter carriers and show the pictures. Talk about the idea of communication, that although people talk to one another, they also write letters to one another and send packages to one another through the mail. Explain that the workers at the post office help us. Encourage the children to describe what they know of their local post office and letter carrier (what he or she wears, drives, carries, and so on).

2. Tell the children to think about the following questions as you ask them and to say how they feel about each. Acknowledge each answer with an encouraging remark:

   Do you think it is better for a letter carrier to walk or drive? Why do you think that?

   If you had something you wanted to tell a friend, would you rather call on the phone or (have an adult) write a letter and mail it? Why would that be better?

   Would you rather be a postal worker or a firefighter? Why? Now you can see why it is important for us to have both.

   Are you more like a letter or a book? Why?

   If you were a letter carrier and it were a rainy day, would you go out and deliver the mail or would you stay home? Why?

   If a letter carrier were walking along and dropped a letter and you saw it, what would you do about it? Why?

Variation/Way to Extend:

• Invite a parent or other person with a stamp collection to visit the school and share the hobby with the children. (**Note:** The collector should understand young children and spend time showing unusually colorful animal-oriented or action-filled stamps. Perhaps an overhead projector could be used to enlarge the stamps so that everyone may see them at one time. The next day, have the children dictate a thank-you letter from them. Let them observe you address, seal, and stamp the envelope. If possible, walk as a group to a nearby mailbox and mail it.)

III-173 SEND IT TO MY HOUSE

Subject Area: Language Arts

Concept/Skill: Verbalizes full name and address

Objectives: The children will recall their full names and addresses and produce pictures or messages to be mailed to their own homes.

Materials:
- Stamped postcards
- Markers

Procedure:

1. Assist each child in verbalizing his or her own full name and address. Demonstrate to each child how you are addressing the postcard to him or her. On the back of the postcard, let each child make a drawing or dictate a message for you to write. Mail the postcards.

2. Allow a few days for delivery, then have a follow-up discussion with the children about receiving the cards at home. Ask, "How did the letter carrier know exactly which card belonged to each child's home?" "What did your parents say about receiving this mail?"

Variation/Way to Extend:

- Teach the following action poem to the children:

  I work for the post office (*pretend to walk from the post office*)
  My mailbag on my back, (*pretend to carry mail on back*)
  I go to all the houses (*pretend to go up to a house*)
  Leaving letters from my sack. (*pretend to drop letters into a mailbox*)
  One, two, three, four, (*hold up fingers to count*)
  Who are these letters for? (*hold pretend letters and scratch head*)
  One for (name) and one for (name) (*pretend to hand out letters*)
  One for (name) and one for you! (*pretend to hand out letters*)

III-174 PAINTING MAIL TRUCKS

Subject Area: Art

Concepts/Skills: Develops fine motor movement of painting
Explores
Is creative

Objective: The children will paint pictures of mail trucks at the easel.

Materials:
- Blue and white paints
- Brushes
- Paper
- Easels
- Pictures
- Mail truck shapes
- Paste

Procedure:

1. Provide pictures of mail trucks (from a set or in a book) to show the children. Use these as a stimulus for the children to paint at the easel. Display the finished paintings around the room.

2. Give each child a mail truck shape to color at the table and then paste onto a background paper. Display these pictures, too.

Variation/Way to Extend:

- Make letter holders as gifts for parents. Have each child color two paper plates. Assist the children in cutting one in half and punching holes around both. Then have the children lace the plates together with colored yarn. Write "Letters" on the bottom section.

III-175   HERE'S OUR NEIGHBORHOOD

Subject Area: Math

Concepts/Skills: Points to and names a triangle, circle, square, rectangle, and diamond
Connects a dotted outline to make a shape
Cuts on a line

Objectives: The children will draw and cut shapes to simulate a neighborhood and match these to their addresses on envelopes.

Materials:
- Colored paper
- Markers
- Scissors
- Addressed envelope for each child
- White crayon
- Tape
- Wall space

Procedure:

1. Take small pieces of colored paper and form triangles, circles, squares, rectangles, and diamonds by outlining one shape on each sheet in dots.

2. Pass these around to the children and instruct them to connect the dots with a marker. Then distribute scissors and have the children cut out their shapes by cutting on the lines.

3. Make a wall display by using the shapes to form a neighborhood. For example, the squares could be the houses; the circles, ponds or parks; the diamonds, ball fields; the triangles, important local points of interest; and the rectangles, stores and offices. Write a child's address on each square and arrange the neighborhood. You might also include black strips of paper for streets and have these correspond to the children's addresses by writing the street names in white crayon.

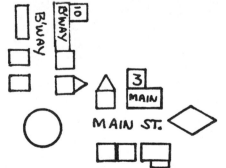

4. Have the children point to and name the various shapes. Then give each child an envelope with his or her address written on it and ask each child to match this to his or her house on the wall.

Variation/Way to Extend:

- For a close-up look at many other occupations, as well as clear photographs of women in nontraditional roles, show the children the book *Butcher, Baker, Cabinetmaker: Photographs of Women at Work,* text by Wendy Saul and photography by A. Heyman (New York: Harper & Row, 1978).

SUMMER

- ○ The Ocean, Rivers, and Lakes
- ○ Insects
- ○ Day and Night
- ○ Vacation and Travel

Weekly Subtheme: The Ocean, Rivers, and Lakes

III–176   OCEAN OR LAND?

Subject Area: Thinking Games

Concepts/Skills: Retells a short story of five sentences in sequence using own words
Labels pictures
Classifies objects

Objectives: The children will identify pictures and classify them accurately.

Materials:
- Wooden dowel
- String
- Pictures
- Tape
- Paper clips
- Oaktag
- Magnet

Procedure:

1. Tell the children to listen carefully to your short story about a girl at the beach. Afterward, ask individual children to tell it back to you in his or her own words.

   "Mandy went to the seashore on a bright, sunny day. She found many colorful shells on the sandy beach. In her pail, she put shiny black mussel shells and white clam shells. When she got home, she glued the shells all over some stiff cardboard. It made a pretty design."

2. Continue a discussion of the seashore. Ask the children about what they can see and do there.

3. Make a fishing pole out of a wooden dowel and string and tie a magnet to the end. On the floor, spread out eight to ten pictures, half of them related to the ocean (shells, fish, crabs, boats, lobsters, whales, sharks, and so on) and half related to the land (trees, cars, buildings, and so on). Attach a paper clip to each picture and allow each child to "fish." As each picture is pulled in, ask the children to identify it and also say in which category (ocean or land) it belongs.

4. Write "Ocean" and "Land" on a piece of oaktag and tape each picture under the appropriate category.

Variations/Ways to Extend:

- Spread a variety of paper fish (with paper clips attached) of different colors on the floor. Allow the children to fish and sort on the basis of different colors.
- Use seashells to sort by size and then let the children paint them.

III–177   OCEAN MONTAGE

Subject Area: Art

Concepts/Skills: Uses scissors with control to cut along a curved line
Expresses self creatively

Objective: The children will construct an ocean montage of pre-cut and original drawings.

Materials:
- Magazines, travel brochures, and so on
- Scissors
- Crayons
- Paste
- Construction paper

Procedure:

1. Ask the children to search through magazines, travel brochures, and so on for pictures of oceans, beaches, and sea life. Have the children cut out their pictures.
2. Create ocean montages by encouraging each child to paste his or her pictures on a large sheet of construction paper. Let the children also include their own drawings of ocean objects and animals.
3. Display the montages at the children's eye-level.

Variations/Ways to Extend:

- Let the children add texture to the montages by spreading glue on the paper and sprinkling with sand. When the glue is dry, shake off the excess sand.
- For background music while the children are creating the montage, play "Summer Day Suite" by Prokofiev (RCA Victor Basic Record Library, 72 Fifth Avenue, New York, NY 10011).

III-178   HUNGRY FISH

Subject Area: Math

Concept/Skill: Understands that each number is one more than the preceding number

Objective: The children will count five fish as they are eaten.

Materials: • Fish-shaped crackers
            • Paper cups

Procedure:

1. Say, "Once upon a time there was a great big fish who loved to swim in the ocean looking for little fish to eat."
2. Distribute five fish-shaped crackers in a paper cup to each child. Tell the children to pick up one fish in each hand and (while sitting in place) show how the fish swim in the ocean. Then say, "Along came the great big fish looking very hungry and ate *one* of your fish." Have each child eat one cracker. Then say, "How many fish did the big fish eat?" (Children should respond, "One.") Continue, saying, "The great big fish was still hungry so it decided to eat another fish." Have the children eat a second cracker.
3. Continue having the children count to five so that all the fish are eaten.

Variations/Ways to Extend:

• Cut out fifteen small fish pictures for each child. Give each child a piece of paper numbered from 1 to 5 down the left side. Guide each child in pasting the appropriate number of fish to the right of each numeral.
• Read the Caldecott Medal book *The Little Island* by Golden MacDonald and Leonard Weisgard (New York: Doubleday, 1946).
• Obtain free (advertising) posters of jumping dolphins, along with a general elementary information brochure, by writing to Marineland of Florida, Box 122, St. Augustine, FL 32086.

III-179 OCEAN MOVEMENTS

Subject Area: Creative Dramatics and Movement

Concept/Skill: Moves body creatively upon teacher's direction

Objective: The children will demonstrate creative body movements as related to the ocean.

Materials:
- Record player (optional)
- Records (optional)

Procedure:

1. You might want to play some background music during this activity. Ask the children to sit on the floor, at least two feet from one another. Say, "Close your eyes and see the ocean in your mind. Picture the waves as they splash up on the sand. See yourself running on the sand and along the water. Now you are playing with a friend, splashing and kicking the waves as they roll in. See yourself playing in the sand. What are you building? (Children can respond with their eyes still closed.) Say goodbye to your friend and open your eyes slowly."

2. Ask the children to stand and perform creative movement following your directions:

   Pretend you are a crab walking along the sand and into the ocean.

   Pretend you are a plane or helicopter flying over the ocean and looking down at the waves.

   Pretend that a wave is coming at you. Get out of the way.

   Pretend you are a hermit crab getting into a shell.

   Pretend you are running into the water and it is very warm or icy cold.

   Pretend you are standing in sand and you draw a letter.

   Pretend you are swimming in the ocean. (Pause). It suddenly becomes a big mattress.

   Pretend you are an ocean wave.

   Pretend you are a boat sailing in the ocean.

Variation/Way to Extend:

- Read *What Does the Tide Do?* by Jean Kinney (Reading, MA: Addison-Wesley, 1966).

III–180 BOAT PARTY

Subject Area: Nutrition and Foods Experience

Concept/Skill: Uses crayons with control

Objectives: The children will draw an edible boat and create one from nutritious foods.

Materials:
- Pictures
- Paper
- Crayons
- Toothpicks
- Apple slices
- Four-inch piece of celery for each child
- Triangular piece of cheese for each child

Procedure:

1. Show the children a variety of pictures of boats moving on the ocean, lakes, and rivers. Discuss how boats (with motors, sails, oars, and so on) move on these bodies of water.

2. Distribute paper and crayons to the children and ask them to draw a new kind of boat—one that would be delicious to eat. As they draw, allow them to dictate what types of foods make up the parts of the boat. Write the names of the foods on the drawing.

3. Once the drawings are completed, tell the children that they are going to create their own boat that they will actually eat. Give each child a four-inch piece of celery. Place a slice of apple in the middle of the celery and assist the children in placing a toothpick through both. At the top of the toothpick, have the child place a triangular piece of cheese.

4. Encourage the children to make up stories about their boats, such as where they may travel to, and so on. Once finished, allow the children to eat their boats, being careful of the toothpicks.

Variations/Ways to Extend:

- Organize a socio-dramatic play experience. Encourage the children to use blocks as small and big boats. Assign the roles of captain and passengers and create a situation, such as "The boat is lost" or "A passenger is sick."
- Write down the stories the children made up about their boats and send these home for families to enjoy reading.

III–181 IDENTIFYING INSECTS

Subject Area: Science

Concept/Skill: Names insects

Objective: The children will identify insects from pictures and a book.

Materials:
- Pictures
- Book
- Preserved insects in plastic vials (optional)

Procedure:

1. Show pictures of insects (or display preserved insects). Pictures of insects can be obtained from the National Audubon Society, 950 Third Avenue, New York, NY 10022. Pictures of insects and spiders can also be obtained from Society for Visual Education, 1345 Diversey Parkway, Chicago, IL 61614.
2. Name each insect (bee, mosquito, ladybug, cricket, grasshopper, ant, butterfly, wasp, moth, fly, and so on) as it is shown.
3. Check around the yard and locate a few places where the children can see insects. Explain that insects have six legs (spiders are not insects because they have eight legs) and antennae, and most have wings. Also explain that insects have no bones, so their bodies are very soft. Their "hard parts" are on the *outside* of their bodies.
4. Read *Everyday Insects* by Gertrude E. Allen (Boston: Houghton-Mifflin, 1963). (**Note:** Although this book is out of print, a copy may be available in your library.) Have the children name the insects as you read the book.

Variation/Way to Extend:

- Using a flannelboard and felt-backed pictures or drawings, show the head (with antennae), thorax, and abdomen, which together make up an insect. Allow the children to come up to the flannelboard and put the pieces together to construct insects. Offer parts for a fly, grasshopper, bee, and so on.

III-182   MOVING LIKE INSECTS

Subject Area: Creative Dramatics and Movement

Concepts/Skills: Moves body creatively upon teacher's direction
Stops movement activity upon teacher's direction

Objective: The children will move like insects, stopping upon the teacher's command.

Materials: • Drum
• Drumstick

Procedure:

1. Position the children around the room. Tell them to pretend that they are insects:

   Move your head and antennae around.
   Remember, you have six legs. Pretend you're walking with six legs.
   You may have wings, too, so fly around.
   Now move around like a very tired insect.

2. At this point, use a drum and drumstick to create a beat while giving directions:

   Keep moving around. You are not tired anymore, but you are very hungry. You are looking for some other insects to eat.
   When the beat stops, freeze and become a beautiful butterfly. (Pause.) FREEZE!
   (Continue the beat.) When the beat stops, freeze into the funniest position you can think of. (Ask them why the positions are funny.) (Pause.) FREEZE!
   When the beat starts, imagine that you are an insect, such as a ladybug, whose job is looking after the farmer's crops. (Continue beat.) You're flying around with your friends, having a good time. (Allow them to play.) Remember to freeze when the beat stops. (Pause.) FREEZE!
   Suddenly you look down and see a bunch of insects attacking fruit trees and vegetable plants. You fly down to chase them away. (Continue the beat.)
   Hooray! You chased away the bad insects and protected the farmer's fruits and vegetables.

3. Conclude the activity by serving a snack of sliced fruits and raw vegetables.

Variation/Way to Extend:

• Play the song "Flight of the Bumble Bee" by Rimsky-Korsakov from the album *Children's Concert Series* (Children's Record Guild).

III–183 HELPFUL AND HARMFUL INSECTS

Subject Area: Social Studies

Concept/Skill: Shows empathy toward other children

Objectives: The children will identify which insects are helpful and harmful and will demonstrate helpful behaviors.

Material: • Pictures

Procedure:

1. Show the children pictures of insects that can be helpful: bee (makes honey); butterfly (pretty to look at); praying mantis (eats insects that harm crops); ladybug (eats insects that harm crops). Discuss what it means to be helpful.

2. Then show pictures of insects that can be harmful: grasshopper (eats crops); bee (stings); mosquito (bites people and may carry disease). Discuss what it means to be harmful to others.

3. Play the game "I Can Do Something Helpful for You." Have the children sit in a circle. Ask each child to stand and show a helpful behavior, such as getting a cup of juice for another child.

Variations/Ways to Extend:

- Have the children choose their favorite helpful insect and draw pictures.
- Read the poem "Bumblebee" (and others) by Margaret W. Brown, found in her book *Nibble, Nibble* (Reading, MA: Addison-Wesley, 1959).

III-184   MUSICAL INSECTS

Subject Areas: Music and Movement

Concepts/Skills: Recalls information previously taught
Compares two objects in terms of sameness and difference

Objective: The children will identify pictures of insects.

Materials: • Laminated pictures
• Record
• Record player

Procedure:

1. In a circle on the floor, place laminated pictures of the insects the children have been discussing. Place as many pictures as there are children.

2. Play a song that is about insects, such as "Shoo Fly." As the music plays, have the children move around the outside of the pictures. When the music stops, have the children sit on the nearest picture. Ask each child to identify the insect. (**Note:** Do not eliminate the children. Four-year-olds do not understand elimination and enjoy the scramble to find and sit on a picture.)

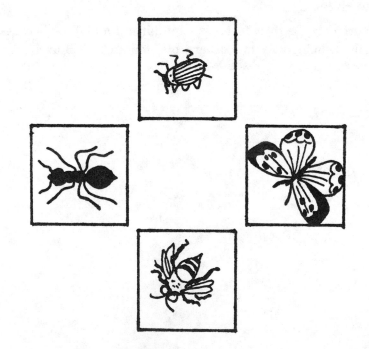

3. Next, encourage the children to move and sound like the insect he or she is sitting on, such as "buzz" like a bee. Ask each child to give one idea about the insect. Also ask the children how a bee and a butterfly are the same and how they are different.

Variation/Way to Extend:

• Sing the song "Beetletown" (see the next page) to the children. Teach them the words and sing it together several times.

Beetletown

Words and Music by **BOB MESSANO**
Arranged by John Sheehan

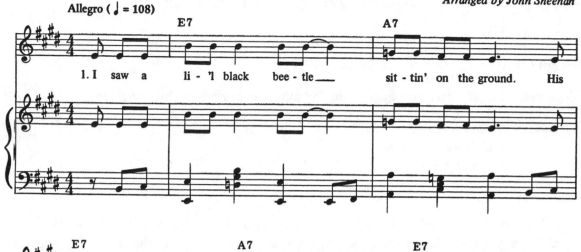

1. I saw a li - 'l black bee - tle___ sit - tin' on the ground. His

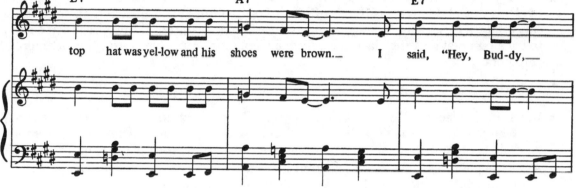

top hat was yel-low and his shoes were brown.__ I said, "Hey, Bud-dy,__

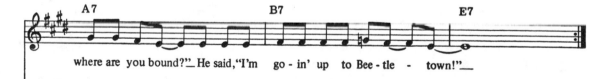

where are you bound?"__ He said,"I'm go - in' up to Bee - tle - town!"__

© 1986 by The Center for Applied Research in Education, Inc.

Copyright 1984 Bob Messano

2. We're gonna have a dance at the old stone wall,
   with buttercup tea and honey for all.
   It's the one and only "Beetle Ball"
   Over in Beetletown!

3. I hope the blackbird doesn't spoil our fun,
   Then we can dance until the mornin' sun.
   We'll go home when the dancin' is done,
   Over in Beetletown!

4. I met a lady beetle sittin' by the door,
   She said, "You don't need a ticket if you can count to four!"
   The next thing you know, I was dancin' across the floor—
   Over in Beetletown!

III-185   PRINT BUTTERFLIES

Subject Area: Art

Concept/Skill: Explores new technique

Objectives: The children will fingerpaint and take monoprints of their creations.

Materials:
- Glazed paper
- Butterfly shapes
- Fingerpaints

Procedure:

1. Encourage the children to fingerpaint on wet, glazed paper in a multitude of colors.
2. Then give each child a fresh sheet of paper that has been cut in the shape of a large butterfly. Have the children press these onto their fingerpaintings and then peel them off. The result will be a monoprint (an impression of their original paintings). Encourage some children to try a bumblebee using black and yellow fingerpaints or a ladybug using black and red fingerpaints.

Variations/Ways to Extend:

- Read the Caldecott Medal book *Frog Went A-Courtin',* retold by John Langstaff and Feodor Rojankovsky (New York: Harcourt Brace Jovanovich, 1955). The story is from an old English/Scottish ballad, and the book contains many humorous pictures of insects.
- After the paintings have dried, give the children black "body" parts cut from paper to glue down the centers and pipe cleaners to glue on as antennae.

Weekly Subtheme: Day and Night

III-186 SUN MURAL

Subject Area: Art

Concepts/Skills: Makes a choice
Explores new technique
Develops fine motor movements of painting, cutting, and pasting

Objective: The children will paint, cut, and paste to construct a wall mural that shows the uses of the sun.

Materials:
- Roll of thin white vinyl
- Tape
- Orange, yellow, and gold acrylic paints
- Magazine pictures
- Scissors

Procedure:

1. Since much of your program will probably take place outdoors this month, try to designate as an outdoor mural a wall adjacent to your playground. Tape the vinyl to the wall. Make a big sun the focal point and let it have triangles emanating from it to demonstrate radiance. Have each child fill in one of these sections with bright yellow, gold, or orange paint.

2. Have the children cut out pictures showing what goes on in the sunshine, such as farming, drying clothes, playing outdoors, swimming, clouds forming, growing fruit, wind blowing, and so on. Tape these around the sun picture to form the mural.

Variations/Ways to Extend:

- If a wall is not available for the mural, make a fence painting by using clothespins to pin the vinyl to the fence.
- Add texture to the mural by pasting yarn over lines in the pictures or on the sun for emphasis.
- Play a recording of the "Overture from William Tell" by Rossini (Angel Records). Let the children pretend to be the sun rising when the music is slow and a storm when the music is fast.

III–187 HOT BALLOONS

Subject Area: Science

Concepts/Skills: Shows an increasing curiosity and sense of adventure
Understands that air takes up space

Objective: The children will conclude that the sun causes air to be warmed and to expand by observing it happen.

Materials:
- Balloons
- Air pump
- Glass soda bottle
- Saucepan
- Water
- Heat source

Procedure:

1. Discuss with the children the idea that the sun is a star and is very hot and very bright. It provides us with light and warmth. It draws moisture up into the clouds, and so, in a way, the sun makes it rain! This allows plants and animals to grow and provides food for us. The sun also heats air and causes it to expand.

2. Use a pump to blow up a balloon (your breath will be too warm to allow these results), and then tie a knot in it. Now step outside into the hot summer sun with the balloon. Have the children notice the balloon expand; it might even break.

3. Demonstrate this point further by placing a balloon over the top of a glass soda bottle. Place the bottle in a saucepan of water and heat the water. (**Caution:** Be sure the children stay away from the heat.) Heating the air in the bottle will cause the balloon to expand.

Variation/Way to Extend:

- Collect some interesting pictures of the sun, moon, stars, and of daylight and nightfall. Mount these on oaktag and cover with clear self-stick vinyl. Then cut each picture into a ten-piece puzzle for the children to put together.

III–188 SUNSHINE AND SHADOWS

Subject Area: Gross Motor Games

Concepts/Skills: Works and plays cooperatively
Moves

Objectives: The children will generalize about differences in temperature between sun and shade and apply recognition of shadows to outdoor games.

Materials: • Large outdoor area
• Thermometer

Procedure:

1. Let the children compare sunny areas to shady ones by looking at the difference. Place a thermometer in the sun and then in the shade and encourage the children to notice what happens.

2. Guide the children in making shadows with such found objects as leaves, flowers, grasses, and stones.
3. Teach the children to play "Shadow Tag." The person who is "It" runs to catch someone else's shadow. If he or she touches another's shadow, then that person becomes "It."

Variations/Ways to Extend:

• Try some creative movement exercises outside, suggesting to the children that they show how people feel when it is extremely sunny and hot. Then ask, "How about when it's cold?" "How do you feel in the cool shade?" "How do you look when you're thirsty?"
• Read *What Does the Sun Do?* by Jean Kinney (Reading, MA: Addison-Wesley, 1967). (**Note:** Although this book is out of print, a copy may be available in your library.)

III–189 STAR, FAR!

Subject Area: Language Arts

Concept/Skill: Supplies a rhyming word

Objective: The children will apply recognition of sounds to make up rhyming words.

Materials: • None

Procedure:

1. Use vocabulary related to day and night to stimulate the children to rhyme. Some examples are:

    I can rhyme with *star* (*car, far, tar* . . .)
    I can rhyme with *sun* (*fun, bun, gun* . . .)
    I can rhyme with *moon* (*June, soon, spoon* . . .)
    I can rhyme with *sky* (*fly, dry, why* . . .)
    I can rhyme with *night* (*fight, bright, tight* . . .)

2. Encourage the children to think of their own rhymes, too.

Variations/Ways to Extend:

*   Mount pictures of these words on oaktag and cut each one out. Give them to the children and have them sort the pictures on the basis of sound (all those that rhyme go together).
*   Read the Caldecott Honor book *Hildilid's Night* by Cheli D. Ryan (New York: Macmillan, 1974). It is a story about a woman who tries to chase away the night.

III-190 THE SUN, MOON, AND STARS

Subject Area: Creative Dramatics and Movement

Concepts/Skills: Listens
Moves body creatively upon teacher's direction

Objective: The children will perform movements that portray celestial bodies.

Materials:
- Large open area
- Record player
- Record

Procedure:

1. Warm up by having the children stretch and bend and move to some music. You might play "Simon Says" or "Looby Loo" to have the children focus on moving certain parts of their bodies.
2. Combine listening skills with movement by giving the children a scenario to act out concerning the stars, sun, moon, planets, and so on. Start, for example, by saying, "I am the sun. I am partly covered by clouds. Now the clouds are gone and I am burning brighter, stronger, and hotter!"
3. Continue with "I am the moon—a big, round, full moon. I am silvery and bright in the dark sky. Now I am a half moon. Now I am a quarter moon."
4. Continue with "I am a star shining as part of the Big Dipper in the summer sky at night. I am shiny and bright. Now a piece of me has broken off and becomes a shooting star."
5. Finish with "I am an astronaut, landing and walking on the moon. I must walk very, very slowly. Now we are headed back to planet Earth."

Variations/Ways to Extend:

- Take a field trip to a local planetarium. These are located in museums, in universities, and even in some public school districts.
- Read *The Night Stella Hid the Stars* by Gail Radley (New York: Crown, 1978). (**Note:** Although this book is out of print, a copy may be available in your library.)

III-191 VACATION FEELINGS

Subject Area: Social Studies

Concepts/Skills: Participates in nonverbal imaginative play
Identifies expressions of feelings

Objective: The children will demonstrate facial expressions appropriate to the situation.

Materials: • Prepared paper plates

Procedure:

1. Give each child two paper plates, one with a happy face and the other with a sad face.
2. Ask the children to listen to events that may occur while they are on vacation. Ask the children to raise the sad face if the event would produce sad feelings. Ask them to raise the happy face if the situation is happy. Encourage the children to express the appropriate facial movements as well. Here are sample situations:

   Your parents say, "We are going on vacation tomorrow. We are going to swim and play games all week."

   While in the car, it becomes very hot and you need a drink.

   You were dreaming that your parents are not taking you on vacation and that you have to stay home.

   Your parents take you to the beach or lake, and you play in the sand all day.

   You play some games at a fair and you win a prize—a big stuffed animal.

   You buy an ice cream cone, but the ice cream falls off and lands in the dirt.

   You meet a new friend who has lots of toys.

Variations/Ways to Extend:

- Repeat the activity a second time with a slight change. Tell the children to put down their paper plates and act out each of the situations.
- Read the poem "The Star in the Pail" by David McCord, found in his book *One at a Time* (Boston: Little, Brown, 1977).

III–192   PURPLE BUBBLY

Subject Areas: Math and Nutrition

Concept/Skill: Understands fraction (½)

Objective: The children will create a nutritious summer drink.

Materials:
- Ingredients
- Blender
- Paper cups
- Ice
- Measuring cup
- Straws

Procedure:

1. Tell the children that they are going to make a cool, nutritious summer drink that can also be made both at home and on vacation. Portions for four children can be made using the following ingredients. Explain to the children that two ½ cups are the same as one cup.

   two ½ cups pineapple juice
   one ½ cup grape juice
   two ½ cups yogurt
   one ripe banana

2. Allow the children to measure the ingredients, emphasizing the ½-cup measurements.

3. Mix the ingredients in a blender, add ice, and serve at snack time.

Variation/Way to Extend:

- While they sip their drinks, encourage the children to think about vacations and trips they have had. Let those who want to take turns telling about these.

Weekly Subtheme: Vacation and Travel

III-193 TRAVELING GAMES

Subject Area: Language Arts

Concepts/Skills: Labels animals
Identifies letters of the alphabet

Objective: The children will play two games that can be played in a vehicle on their way to a vacation.

Materials: • Pictures (optional)

Procedure:

1. Teach the children games they can play with their parents or siblings while traveling in a car, train, bus, or plane on their way to a vacation spot.
   Circus—Each player identifies animals (either an actual animal or from a picture on a sign) and claims that animal as part of his or her circus. (**Note:** You might ask the parents to write down the names of the animals for the children.) At the end of the specified time, each player identifies the animals and describes the sound each one makes.
   Alphabet Travel—Starting with the first letter of the alphabet, each player looks for signs with that letter and succeeding letters. As each player spots the letter in a word on a billboard, road sign, or license plate, it is claimed as his or her letter.
2. When playing these games in class, you might want to post pictures of animals and signs around the room and keep track of the animals and letters claimed.

Variation/Way to Extend:

• Give the children an assortment of cut-out letters that are thick enough (about 1/16 of an inch) to produce a raised impression. Let them choose whatever letters they want with which to work (to form a word or their name). Have each child place a sheet of stiff paper over the letters and rub with the side of a fat crayon. Watch the letters appear!

III-194 CAMPING VACATION

Subject Area: Creative Dramatics and Movement

Concept/Skill: Participates in imaginative play

Objectives: The children will identify equipment used for camping and engage in socio-dramatic play.

Materials:
- Large blanket
- Prop box
- Fishing props
- String
- Red cellophane
- Flashlight

Procedure:

1. Explore the topic of camping while on vacation and encourage socio-dramatic play by organizing a camping site either inside or outside the school. Create a home-made tent by using a large blanket (inside, tie the blanket around several chairs; outside, attach the blanket between two trees). Create a camping prop box consisting of the following materials: canteen, lantern, flashlight, compass, cooking utensils, toothbrush, snacks, pillows, blankets (sleeping bags are optional), and pajamas.

2. Use red cellophane along with a flashlight to create a pretend campfire. Allow the children to pretend fishing, using wooden sticks, string, magnets, and paper cut-outs of fish with paper clips attached.

3. Assist the children in developing camping themes, such as waking up, cooking, fishing, and going to sleep.

Variations/Ways to Extend:

- Arrange for the children to visit a store to look at camping supplies.
- Make a camping snack consisting of peanuts, raisins, and cereal.

III-195 VIEW THROUGH A PORTHOLE!

Subject Area: Art

Concepts/Skills: Reproduces shapes
Controls brush and paint
Uses scissors with control

Objectives: The children will construct paper portholes by painting, cutting, and pasting.

Materials:
- Two paper plates for each child
- Scissors
- Watercolors
- Brushes
- Plastic wrap
- Construction paper
- String
- Glue
- Markers
- Tape

Procedure:

1. Talk about going to a lake or seashore for vacation. Encourage each child to paint an impressionistic underwater scene (water, rocks, seaweed, coral, and so on) on one paper plate.
2. Help each child cut a large circle out of the center of the other plate. Cover this hole with plastic wrap and tape it in place on the inside of the plate.
3. Next, have the children draw or trace a few small sea animals (fish, starfish, clams, and so on) on construction paper and cut them out. Glue these onto short lengths of string and glue the other end of the string to the top of the painted paper plate so that the fish hang in front of the scene.
4. Glue the two paper plates together and enjoy the view through the porthole.

Variations/Ways to Extend:

- Show the children pictures of boats, such as sailboats and motorboats. Have the children define a space in the room as a sailboat and use sticks, string, blocks, sheets of paper, and tape to build it. Make tickets allowing passengers aboard. Encourage dramatic play.
- Play a recording of "Play on the Beach" by Mompou from the album *Pictures from Childhood* (RCA Victor Basic Record Library, 72 Fifth Avenue, New York, NY 10011).

APPENDIX

SPECIAL SECTION
FOR PRESCHOOL DIRECTORS

Directors who use the *Preschool Curriculum Activities Library* will have a strong rationale to support their choices of topics and activities with children of different ages. Those who have implemented this curriculum can easily demonstrate how activities dealing with the same topic can be developmentally different and therefore appropriate for children who vary in age.

Directors are often asked by parents of home-bound children if activities are available from the school that the parent can use at home to teach the child. Again, the learning experiences in this book can be offered to parents to reduce fears about their children "missing" a preschool experience.

As parents become more sophisticated regarding their choice of a preschool, they may ask to see the curriculum. Parents can be shown how themes and topics incorporate many different skills and age-appropriate experiences. Such a rationale provides a clear understanding of the school's direction and creates a sense of integration and purpose for children, parents, and staff.

At its best, curriculum development is an ongoing process. Therefore, modify the themes and daily activities to meet the local and geographic needs of your children. The changes made, however, will be within a coherent framework so that each child, starting at age two, will be able to build upon the skills and knowledge earlier gained.

Described below are six steps to follow when creating or improving a preschool curriculum. It is suggested that a team of teachers address the questions following each step. New learning experiences can be created that complement and support the activities found in the *Library,* providing a well-rounded curriculum based on a planned approach.

Step 1: DETERMINE BELIEFS ABOUT HOW CHILDREN LEARN

According to Jones (1981), there are two basic approaches to creating curriculum for young children:

Approach 1—create activities based on children's interests
Approach 2—create activitites based on what children need to know

Proponents of Approach #1 believe that preschool children learn through direct experience, in their own creative ways, using real, natural objects. Preschoolers are in what Jean Piaget (1952) has called the "preoperational stage"; they thrive on free choice and manipulation of concrete objects in a stimulating environment. Also, Approach #1 advocates believe that abstract language in young children is largely undeveloped and therefore teachers should keep verbalizations such as questions and conveyance of facts to a minimum.

Proponents of Approach #2, however, argue that a curriculum based on concrete experiences, with a minimum of teacher "talk", is difficult to justify. Instead, it is felt that children must be prepared for living in an American culture which places much importance on verbal skill and high test scores. Approach #2, therefore, places emphasis on teacher conveyance of information and development of the children's ability to recall that information.

The curriculum presented in the *Library* offers a *combination* of both approaches. Learning experiences have been devised that are of high interest to children and encourage them to construct, move, and interact, while providing teachers with the opportunity to communicate information in an appropriate manner. It is clear that preschool children need direct, concrete, and high-interest experiences along with well-timed guidance and instruction. A combination of both approaches is essential to building an effective preschool curriculum.

Questions for Teachers

1. Which approach does your school follow?
2. Are there enough concrete experiences?
3. Is there opportunity for teacher conveyance of information?
4. What changes should be made?

Step 2: SELECT LONG-RANGE GOALS FOR THE CHILDREN

Four long-range early childhood goals are listed below. The activities described in the *Library* are based on these goals.

- Competence—to develop children's ability in the areas of language, numbers, and interest in books
- Cooperation—to enhance *self-concept* and *other-concept* through group activity and sharing experiences
- Autonomy—to encourage children to initiate, ask questions, and make limited choices
- Creativity—to construct new products, think of new ideas, and find alternative solutions

Questions for Teachers

1. Are the learning experiences you've created directed at achieving the four goals?
2. Is each goal approached through a variety of activities?

Step 3: ASSESS CHILDREN'S SKILLS-CONCEPTS NEEDS

The foundation of preschool curriculum planning is the observation and assessment of the individual needs of children. The Skills-Concepts Checklist found in this book can be duplicated, placed in each child's folder, and used to evaluate his or her progress during January and June of the school year. Anecdotal comments can be added to a child's folder to assist teachers in determining the skills that he or she has learned or that need to be strengthened.

Questions for Teachers

1. Do you take enough time to observe each child and record significant observations?
2. Do you keep a file folder on each child, containing the Checklist and anecdotal information?

3. Do you use your observations to make curricular changes?
4. How can the Checklist be modified to reflect special skills appropriate to your population of children?

Step 4: CREATE DEVELOPMENTALLY APPROPRIATE ACTIVITIES

All of the activities described in the *Library* are designed to achieve the long-range goals stated in Step 2 and develop the competencies found in the Skills-Concepts Checklist. Each learning experience develops one or more skills or concepts and is related to one of the six general content areas deemed appropriate for preschool children by Hildebrand (1980):

- The Child (personal data; health; body parts; relationship to family, school, and the world)
- The Community (people, workers, institutions, traditions)
- World of Plants (beauty, food)
- World of Machines (vehicles, small machines)
- World of Animals (pleasure, food)
- Physical Forces in World (weather)

Each activity in the *Library* is categorized into one of the following subject areas:

Language Arts	Art
Science	Music
Nutrition/Foods Experience	Math
Creative Dramatics/Movement	Thinking Games
Social Studies	Gross Motor Games

The children's learning can be further enhanced through additional field trips; the creation of learning experiences; and the use of traditional preschool materials and equipment such as blocks, sand, water, and paint (Seefeldt, 1980). The activities should be implemented in a classroom environment that, according to Harms and Clifford (1980), contains four characteristics:

- *Predictable* (well-defined activity centers, noisy and quiet areas, and labeled items)
- *Supportive* (child-sized equipment, play-alone space, and self-selection in activities)
- *Reflective* (children's artwork displayed, and multicultural and nonsexist materials)
- *Varied* (balance of active and quiet times, and indoor and outdoor play)

Questions for Teachers
1. Can the activities created and implemented by the staff be justified based on age-appropriateness?
2. How can the activities, themes, and subthemes found in this book be modified to fit the interests and needs of your children?
3. Are learning centers appropriately equipped?
4. Is the class environment predictable, supportive, reflective, and varied?

Step 5: PLAN FOR REPETITION OF CONCEPTS

Skills and concepts learned by young children need to be reinforced and extended. Many early childhood experts agree that facts must be placed into a structural pattern or frame of reference; otherwise, they will be forgotten. The pattern of activities found in this curriculum follows the model of primary and secondary reinforcement as described by Harlan (1980).

Harlan believes that concepts are built slowly from many simple facts or instances that can be generalized into a unifying idea. She recommends that teachers use her idea of *primary reinforcement* by creating a variety of activities (stories, fingerplays, songs, art, creative movement, math, food experiences, and so on) and by consciously reinforcing a concept or skill throughout each learning experience.

The curriculum presented here allows children to study one topic each week and be exposed to one of the ten subject areas (listed in Step 4) each day. By creating five different activities around one topic, the teacher has the opportunity to reinforce and extend concepts and skills.

Questions for Teachers

1. Are skills and concepts learned in one activity reinforced in other activities?
2. Can further activities be created that reinforce existing learning experiences?

Step 6: EVALUATE THE CHILDREN'S PROGRESS

Teachers can effectively evaluate the success of each activity by reviewing each lesson's stated behavioral objective and concepts/skills to be learned. They can then ask the question, "To what extent did each child learn what we intended to be learned?" Anecdotal notes can be briefly written and the Checklist can be used regarding each child's demonstrated behavior and skill acquisition. Decisions can be made providing for individual assistance or creating a new activity to reinforce a skill that a child may have had difficulty acquiring.

Questions for Teachers

1. When will the staff take some time (immediately after an activity, before lunch, after school) to evaluate what the children have learned?
2. What provisions can be made to assist children in acquiring certain skills?

REFERENCES

Harlan, Jean, *Science Experiences for the Early Childhood Years.* Columbus, Ohio: Chas. E. Merrill, 1980.

Harms, Thelma, and Richard M. Clifford, *Early Childhood Environmental Rating Scale.* New York Teacher's College Press, 1980.

Hildebrand, Verna, *Introduction to Early Childhood Education.* Columbus, Ohio: Chas. E. Merrill, 1980.

Jones, Edwin, *Dimensions of Teaching-Learning Environments: Handbook for Teachers.* Pasadena, Calif.: Pacific Oaks College Press, 1981.

Piaget, Jean, *The Origins of Intelligence in Children.* New York: International Universities Press, 1952.

Seefeldt, Carol, *Teaching Young Children.* Englewood Cliffs, N.J.: Prentice-Hall, 1980.

COMPLETE PRESCHOOL
DEVELOPMENT PLAN

SKILLS-CONCEPTS CHECKLIST*
FOR TWO-YEAR-OLDS
(Developmental Characteristics)

A child who is 24 to 36 months of age tends to develop skills rapidly. The following abilities will emerge as the child approaches age three. The activities within this book have been designed to develop the skills and concepts listed below in a manner consistent with the child's needs and interests. Monitor the child's progress and evaluate it twice during the school year by placing a check (√) next to the skill or concept once it has been mastered.

Name _____ Birthdate _____

COGNITIVE

Personal Curiosity/Autonomy	JAN.	JUNE
1. Shows curiosity and interest in surroundings		
2. Imitates the actions of adults		
3. Imitates play of other children		
4. Finds own play area or activity		
5. Enjoys looking at books		
6. Begins to notice differences between safe and unsafe environments (2½ to 3)		

Senses		
7. Begins to develop senses of touch, smell, taste, and hearing		
8. Begins to place large puzzle pieces in appropriate slots		

Memory		
9. Refers to self by name		
10. Points to common object on command		
11. Associates use with common objects		
12. Stacks three rings by size		
13. Knows that different activities go on at different times of the day (2½ to 3)		
14. Understands the idea of waiting for someone else to go first (2½ to 3)		

Creativity		
15. Shows simple symbolic play (pretends block is a cup)		
16. Acts out a simple story (2½ to 3)		
17. Draws a face (no arms or legs) (2½ to 3)		

Comments:

* This Checklist was developed from the *Skill-Concept Development Checklists for Two Through Five Year Olds* (St. Louis County, Missouri: Parent-Child Early Education). Developed by the Ferguson-Florissant School District. Parts reprinted with their permission.

© 1986 by The Center for Applied Research in Education, Inc.

LANGUAGE

Sentence Structure	JAN.	JUNE
18. Describes what happened in two or three words		
19. Verbalizes wants ("Want water.")		
20. Repeats parts of songs, rhymes, and fingerplays		
21. Gives first and last names when asked (2½ to 3)		
22. Uses short sentences to convey simple ideas (2½ to 3)		

Listening

23. Listens to simple stories and songs		
24. Follows simple directions		
25. Places objects in, on, beside, or under		
26. Identifies loud and soft		

Labeling

27. Identifies own gender		
28. Identifies boy or girl		
29. Identifies self in mirror		
30. Names common objects in pictures		

Comments:

SELF

31. Points to six body parts when named		
32. Puts on and removes coat unassisted		
33. Lifts and drinks from cup and replaces on table		
34. Spoon feeds without spilling		
35. Begins to understand cleanliness		
36. Helps put things away		

Comments:

SOCIAL STUDIES

37. Identifies self from a snapshot		
38. Shows pleasure in dealing with people and things		
39. Values own property and names personal belongings (2½ to 3)		
40. Follows simple rules in a game run by an adult (2½ to 3)		

Comments:

© 1986 by The Center for Applied Research in Education, Inc.

MATH

Counting

	JAN.	JUNE
41. Understands the concept of "one"		
42. Counts two (repeats two digits)		
43. Indicates awareness of more than two (2½ to 3)		

Classifying

44. Groups things together by size (one category) (2½ to 3)		

Size Differences

45. Points to big and little objects (2½ to 3)		

Shapes

46. Differentiates circle and square (2½ to 3)		

Comments:

SCIENCE (2½ to 3)

Concepts

47. Knows the names of three animals		
48. Can associate the words *grass, plants,* and *trees* with correct objects		
49. Identifies rain, clouds, and sun		
50. Begins to understand hard and soft		
51. Begins to understand hot and cold		
52. Begins to understand wet and dry		
53. Matches two color samples		

Comments:

GROSS MOTOR

Arm-Eye Coordination

54. Throws a small object two feet		
55. Catches a rolled ball and rolls it forward		

Body Coordination

56. Jumps with two feet		
57. Claps with music		
58. Walks on tip toe		
59. Walks upstairs alone (both feet on each step) (2½ to 3)		
60. Walks downstairs alone (both feet on each step) (2½ to 3)		
61. Hops on one foot (2½ to 3)		

Comments:

© 1986 by The Center for Applied Research in Education, Inc.

FINE MOTOR

Finger Strength and Dexterity	JAN.	JUNE
62. Fills and dumps containers with sand		
63. Turns single pages (2½ to 3)		

Eye-Hand Coordination		
64. Applies glue and pastes collage pieces		
65. Paints with a large brush		
66. Tears paper		
67. Strings five large beads		
68. Colors with a large crayon		
69. Rolls, pounds, and squeezes clay		
70. Draws a horizontal line		
71. Builds a six-block tower (2½ to 3)		
72. Uses scissors with one hand to cut paper (2½ to 3)		

Comments:

© 1986 by The Center for Applied Research in Education Inc.

SKILLS–CONCEPTS CHECKLIST*
FOR THREE-YEAR-OLDS
(Developmental Characteristics)

A child who is 36 to 48 months of age continues to expand his or her cognitive, affective, and physical growth. The following abilities will emerge as the child approaches age four. The activities within this book have been designed to develop the skills and concepts listed below in a manner consistent with the child's needs and interests. Monitor the child's progress and evaluate it twice during the school year by placing a check (√) next to the skill or concept once it has been mastered.

Name _____ Birthdate _____

COGNITIVE

Personal Curiosity/Autonomy	JAN.	JUNE
1. Shows curiosity and the need to investigate/explore anything new		
2. Asks questions (Who?, What?, Where?, or Why?)		

Senses		
3. Demonstrates accurate sense of touch, smell, and taste		
4. Identifies common sounds		
5. Places objects on their outlines		
6. Observes objects closely		

Memory		
7. Recalls three objects that are visually presented		
8. Identifies what's missing from a picture		
9. Acts out simple everyday activities		

Logical Thinking		
10. Places three pictured events from a familiar story in sequence and expresses each picture sequence in three thoughts		

Relationships		
11. Pairs related objects and pictures, such as shoe and sock		
12. Recognizes which doesn't belong in a group of three items (for example, banana, chair, and apple)		

Creativity		
13. Draws a face with facial parts and stick arms and legs		
14. Dramatizes a simple story		
15. Uses animistic thinking (stuffed animals have human characteristics)		
16. Plays using symbols (objects stand for real objects)		

Comments:

_____

* This checklist was developed from the *Skill–Concept Development Checklists for Two Through Five Year Olds* (St. Louis County, Missouri: Parent–Child Early Education). Developed by the Ferguson–Florissant School District. Parts reprinted with their permission.

© 1986 by The Center for Applied Research in Education, Inc.

LANGUAGE

Sentence Structure	JAN.	JUNE
17. Speaks in four- to six-word sentences		
18. Uses *I, you, me, he,* and *she* correctly		
19. Engages in simple conversation		
20. Memorizes and repeats simple rhymes, songs, or fingerplays of four lines		
21. Understands sentences and questions as indicated by a relevant response		
22. Names plural form to refer to more than one		
23. Describes action in pictures		

Listening

	JAN.	JUNE
24. Listens to short stories and simple poems		
25. Follows two directions		
26. Understands opposites (up/down; open/closed; stop/go; happy/sad; fast/slow; hot/cold)		
27. Understands prepositions (in, out, over, under, on, off, top, bottom, in front of, in back of)		

Labeling

	JAN.	JUNE
28. Names concrete objects in environment		
29. Recognizes and names articles of clothing worn		
30. Recognizes and names pieces of furniture		

Comments:

SELF

	JAN.	JUNE
31. Points to and names body parts (head, hands, arms, knees, legs, chin, feet, and face parts)		
32. Tells own full name, sex, and age		
33. Feels good about self and abilities		

Comments:

SOCIAL STUDIES

Interpersonal

	JAN.	JUNE
34. Enjoys being with other children		
35. Begins learning the give and take of play		
36. Begins participation in a group		

Concepts

	JAN.	JUNE
37. Begins to understand that self and others change		
38. Understands that parental figures care for home and family		
39. Understands that people are alike and different in how they look and feel (3½ to 4)		

Comments:

© 1986 by The Center for Applied Research in Education, Inc.

MATH

Counting	JAN.	JUNE
40. Rote counts to ten		
41. Understands number concepts (when presented with a given number of objects, child can tell how many there are up to six)		

Classifying

42. Sorts objects into two given categories (by size, shape, or color)		

Size Differences

43. Understands concepts of full and empty		
44. Understands big/little; tall/short		

Shapes

45. Points to and labels shapes		
46. Matches shapes (circle, square, triangle, and rectangle)		

Sets

47. Matches sets containing up to five objects		
48. Constructs sets of blocks when given a model		

Comments:

SCIENCE

Concepts

49. Understands that there are many kinds of animals		
50. Understands that animals move in different ways		
51. Understands that most plants make seeds for new plants		
52. Understands that seeds grow into plants with roots, stems, leaves, and flowers		
53. Understands that air is everywhere		
54. Understands that water has weight		

Colors

55. Matches colors		
56. Points to appropriate color upon command		
57. Names three primary colors (red, yellow, and blue)		

Comments:

GROSS MOTOR

Arm–Eye Coordination

58. Catches a large ball from 5- to 8-foot distance		
59. Throws a ball overhand with accuracy from 4- to 6-foot distance		
60. Rolls a large ball to a target		
61. Throws a beanbag at a target five feet away		

© 1986 by The Center for Applied Research in Education, Inc.

Body Coordination

	JAN.	JUNE
62. Walks forward/backward on an 8-foot line		
63. Jumps three jumps with both feet		
64. Hops on one foot two or more times		
65. Moves body in response to simple teacher commands		
66. Walks on tiptoe		
67. Rides a tricycle		
68. Claps with music		

Comments:

FINE MOTOR

Finger Strength and Dexterity

	JAN.	JUNE
69. Makes balls and snakes with clay		
70. Pastes with index finger		

Eye-Hand Coordination

71. Strings at least four half-inch beads		
72. Puts pegs into pegboard		
73. Screws and unscrews nuts, bolts, and lids of various sizes		
74. Holds crayon with fingers rather than fist		
75. Paints with a large brush on large piece of paper		
76. Copies horizontal lines, vertical lines, circles, crosses, diagonal lines		
77. Uses scissors but does not necessarily follow lines		
78. Puts together a six- or seven-piece puzzle		
79. Laces following a sequence of holes		

Comments:

© 1986 by The Center for Applied Research in Education, Inc.

SKILLS–CONCEPTS CHECKLIST*
FOR FOUR-YEAR-OLDS
(Developmental Characteristics)

A child who is 48 to 60 months of age typically demonstrates a large increase in vocabulary and physical abilities. The following abilities will emerge as the child approaches age five. The activities within this book have been designed to develop the skills and concepts listed below in a manner consistent with the child's needs and interests. Monitor the child's progress and evaluate it twice during the school year by placing a check (√) next to the skill or concept once it has been mastered.

Name _____ Birthdate _____

COGNITIVE

Personal Curiosity/Autonomy	JAN.	JUNE
1. Shows an increasing curiosity and sense of adventure		
2. Asks an increasing number of questions		
3. Takes initiative in learning		
4. Shows an interest in the printed word		
5. Pays attention and concentrates on a task		

Senses		
6. Demonstrates accurate sense of touch ("thick" or "thin") and smell		
7. Describes foods by taste (sweet, sour, and salty)		
8. Reproduces a simple pattern of different items from memory		
9. Ranks sounds (loud, louder, loudest; soft, softer, softest)		
10. Observes objects and pictures closely		

Memory		
11. Recalls information previously taught		

Logical Thinking		
12. Interprets the main idea of a story		
13. Orders pictures by time sequence to tell a story		

Relationships		
14. Makes a simple comparison of two objects in terms of difference ("How are a cat and dog different?") and sameness ("How are a cat and dog alike?")		
15. Completes a statement of parallel relationships		

Predicting		
16. Predicts what will happen next in a story or situation		
17. Predicts realistic outcomes of events ("What will happen if we go on a picnic?")		

* This checklist was developed from the *Skill–Concept Development Checklists for Two Through Five Year Olds* (St. Louis County, Missouri: Parent–Child Early Education). Developed by the Ferguson-Florissant School District. Parts reprinted with their permission.

© 1986 by The Center for Applied Research in Education, Inc.

Creativity	JAN.	JUNE
18. Responds well to nondirective questions ("How many ways can you think of to move across the room?")		
19. Proposes alternative ways of doing art experiences, movement activities, and story endings		
20. Represents thoughts in pictures		
21. Draws a human figure with major body parts		
22. Participates verbally or nonverbally in imaginative play or puppetry (socio-dramatic play)		
23. Acts out a familiar story or nursery rhyme as the teacher recites		

Comments:

LANGUAGE

Sentence Structure

	JAN.	JUNE
24. Speaks in six, eight, ten, or more words		
25. Makes relevant verbal contributions in small group discussion		
26. Shows understanding of past, present, and future tenses by using proper verb form		
27. Verbalizes songs and fingerplays		
28. Dictates own experience stories		
29. Describes a simple object using color, size, shape, composition, and use		
30. Describes a picture with three statements		

Listening

31. Listens to directions for games and activities		
32. Listens to stories of at least ten minutes in length		
33. Retells five-sentence short story in sequence using own words		
34. Understands prepositions		

Labeling

35. Labels common everyday items such as clothing, animals, and furniture		
36. Orally labels pictures and drawings ("That's a dog.")		

Letter/Word Recognition

37. Verbally identifies letters in first name (and subsequently in last name)		
38. Identifies many letters of the alphabet		
39. Distinguishes words that begin with the same sound (*book/boy*)		
40. Names two words that rhyme in a group of three (*tie, road, pie*)		
41. Supplies a rhyming word to rhyme with a word given by the teacher		
42. Associates a letter with its sound in spoken words		

Comments:

© 1986 by The Center for Applied Research in Education, Inc.

SELF	JAN.	JUNE
43. Touches, names, and tells function of parts of the body (head, eyes, hands, arms, feet, legs, nose, mouth, ears, neck, trunk, ankle, knee, shoulder, wrist, elbow, and heel)		
44. Verbalizes full name, address, age, birthday, and telephone number		
45. Identifies expressions of feelings		
46. Feels good about self and abilities		

Comments:

	JAN.	JUNE

SOCIAL STUDIES

Interpersonal

	JAN.	JUNE
47. Shows empathy toward other children		
48. Works cooperatively with adults		
49. Works and plays cooperatively with other children		

Concepts

	JAN.	JUNE
50. Begins to understand that problems can be solved by talking and not fighting		
51. Understands that we wear appropriate clothing to protect us from extremes of weather		
52. Understands that families share responsibilities of work and recreation		
53. Begins to understand the importance of keeping the school surroundings clean and free from litter		

Comments:

	JAN.	JUNE

MATH

Counting

	JAN.	JUNE
54. Counts from 1 to _____		
55. Understands ordinal positions first through fifth		
56. Recognizes and orders the cardinal numerals in sequence		
57. Solves simple verbal problems using numerals ("If you have two pieces of candy and I give you one more, how many will you have?")		

Classifying

	JAN.	JUNE
58. Classifies objects by color, size, shape, and texture		

Size Differences

	JAN.	JUNE
59. Orders and compares size differences (big, bigger, biggest; small, smaller, smallest; short, shorter, shortest; long, longer, longest)		

Shapes

	JAN.	JUNE
60. Points to and names: triangle, circle, square, rectangle, and diamond		

© 1986 by The Center for Applied Research in Education, Inc.

Quantitative Concepts	JAN.	JUNE
61. Distinguishes between concepts of "some," "most," and "all"		
62. Compares objects as to weight ("Which is heavier?" "Which is lighter?")		
63. Understands concepts of "full," "half full," and "empty"		
64. Understands fractions (½, ¼, whole)		

Sets

	JAN.	JUNE
65. Identifies a set as a collection of objects having a common property		
66. Establishes a one-to-one correspondence through matching members of equivalent sets (matching six cowboys to six cowboy hats)		
67. Distinguishes between equivalent and non-equivalent sets through matching		
68. Understands that each number is one more than the preceding number ("What is one more than two?")		
69. Identifies an empty set as one having no members		

Comments:

SCIENCE

Concepts

	JAN.	JUNE
70. Understands that each animal needs its own kind of food and shelter		
71. Understands that plants need water, light, warmth, and air to live		
72. Understands that many foods we eat come from seeds and plants		
73. Understands that some things float in water and some things sink in water		
74. Understands the balance of nature—that is, animals need to eat plants, vegetables, and insects in order to live		
75. Understands that plant life, animal life, and other aspects of the environment must be respected		

Colors

	JAN.	JUNE
76. Points to and names colors		

Comments:

GROSS MOTOR

Arm–Eye Coordination

	JAN.	JUNE
77. Catches a ball away from body with hands only (large ball/small ball)		
78. Throws a ball or beanbag with direction		
79. Throws a ball into the air and catches it by self		
80. Bounces and catches a ball		

© 1986 by The Center for Applied Research in Education, Inc.

Body Coordination

	JAN.	JUNE
81. Walks forward and backward on a line ten feet long without stepping off		
82. Walks a line heel-to-toe eight feet long without stepping off		
83. Balances on foot for five seconds		
84. Stops movement activity upon teacher's direction		
85. Moves body creatively upon teacher's direction		
86. Claps with music		

Rhythm

87. Claps and marches in time with music		
88. Responds to rhythms with appropriate body movements		

General Movement

89. Produces the following motions: walks backwards, runs smoothly, marches, skips, gallops, hops four times on each foot, walks heel-to-toe, and walks and runs on tiptoe		

Comments:

FINE MOTOR

Finger Strength and Dexterity

90. Folds and creases paper two times		
91. Folds paper into halves, quarters, and diagonals		

Eye-Hand Coordination

92. Strings ten small beads		
93. Follows a sequence of holes when lacing		
94. Works a puzzle of ten or more pieces		
95. Uses crayon or pencil with control within a defined area		
96. Connects a dotted outline to make a shape		
97. Follows a series of dot-to-dot numerals, 1–10, to form an object		
98. Reproduces shapes (circle, square, triangle, and rectangle)		
99. Controls brush and paint		
100. Uses scissors with control to cut along a straight line and a curved line		

Comments:

© 1986 by The Center for Applied Research in Education, Inc.